Buland Al-Ḥaidari and Modern Iraqi Poetry

BULAND AL-ḤAIDARI

and

MODERN IRAQI POETRY

Selected Poems

BULAND AL-ḤAIDARI

Edited and translated by 'Abdulwāḥid Lu'lu'a

UNIVERSITY OF NOTRE DAME PRESS

NOTRE DAME, INDIANA

University of Notre Dame Press
Notre Dame, Indiana 46556
undpress.nd.edu

Copyright © 2023 by the University of Notre Dame

Published in the United States of America

Library of Congress Control Number: 2022951787

ISBN: 978-0-268-20530-0 (Hardback)
ISBN: 978-0-268-20531-7 (Paperback)
ISBN: 978-0-268-20532-4 (WebPDF)
ISBN: 978-0-268-20529-4 (Epub)

CONTENTS

Introduction   ix

A Note about the Translation of Arabic Poetry   xiii

From *Clay Throb* (1946) خفقة الطين

   1. Semiramis   3

   2. Autumn Echo   9

   3. Whimper   11

   4. Dreaming Silence   13

   5. Boredom   15

   6. Clay Throb   17

   7. Shades   19

   8. Closed Lips   20

From *Songs of the Dead City* (1951) أغاني المدينة الميتة

   9. Barrenness   23

   10. Depths   25

   11. Postman   26

   12. Image   27

   13. Three Signs   30

14. The Hypocritical Wound   32

15. At Night   33

16. Here You Are   34

17. Roads   35

18. Old Age   36

19. Dream   38

20. An Old Love   39

21. Slavery   40

22. O My Friend   41

23. Deceit   42

24. Lost Step   43

25. Loss   45

26. Where To?   46

From *Steps in Exile* (1965) خُطُوات في الغربة

27. Secret   49

28. Old Image   51

29. Judas's Repentance   53

30. You Came with the Dawn   55

31. Bitter Land   57

32. I Want To   58

33. Tomorrow Here   60

34. And Tomorrow I Return   62

35. He Said Something to Us   65

36. Return to Hiroshima   67

37. In a Few Hours   69

38. A Talk for Next Saturday   71

39. The Eighth Journey   73

40. At Forty   74

41. To My Town   75

42. Steps in Exile   77

From *The Journey of Yellow Letters* (1968) رحلة الحروف الصُفر

43. To a Negro from Alabama   81

44. Disappointment of the Man of the Past   83

45. Desolation   84

46. Genesis   86

47. Dreaming of Return   88

48. Two Faces   90

49. Message of the Small Man   92

50. The Paling Salt   94

51. Age of Rubber Stamps   96

52. I Wish If   98

53. Short Laugh   99

54. The Waiting Sails   101

55. Suffocation   102

56. Call of a Nation   104

57. Dream of the Snow   105

58. At the Crossroads   106

59. A Child of the First War   107

60. Night, Cold, and Wardens   109

61. Journey of the Yellow Letters   111

From *Songs of the Tired Guard* (1971)

Introduction   115

62. Sleeping Pills   116

63. Indicted, Though Innocent   119

64. A Call for Stupor   121

65. A Dream in Four Scenes   122

66. Expulsion   124

67. The Killed Witness   125

68. Apology   127

69. Between Two Points   128

70. Dialogue in the Bend   129

71. Confessions from 1961   130

72. Hey . . . You Are Indicted   134

73. Dialogue in Three Dimensions   137

74. Procession of the Seven Sins   152

75. Call of the Seven Sins   154

76. Stolen Frontiers   160

77. Sindbad's Eighth Journey   162

78. On the Verge of the Fallen World   163

79. Two Voices Late at Night   166

80. I Will Stay Here   168

INTRODUCTION

Buland Al-Ḥaidari (192–96) is considered the fourth pillar supporting the dome of modernity in Arabic poetry. Along with the founder of that modernity, Nāzik Al-Malā'ika (1923–2007), were also born in 1926 the two other eminent poets: Badre Shākir Al-Sayyāb and 'Abdulwahhāb Al-Bayyāti. This led some commentators to celebrate the year 1926 as marking the birth of genius in modern Iraqi poetry. But the urge to change and liberate various aspects of life in the mid-1940s, particularly after the end of the Second World War, was felt on various levels of Iraqi society and, understandably, in other Arab societies. Some of those tendencies to liberate and change took the form of rather blasphemous attempts to break away from age-revered traditions. But a healthy desire to change and liberate was seen in the famous female Iraqi poet Nāzik, who, like many intellectuals of her generation, was enamored with the idea of liberty and freedom. As a poet, she started by liberating the "form" of traditional Arabic poetry, based on a line of two hemistiches and a set number of prosodic measures. The logical argument that the poet advanced was that if an idea or image can be expressed by a line of one hemistich with two, three, or even six prosodic measures, there is no need to stick to the traditional two-hemistich line with a set number of measures, which had been canonized by Al-Farāhīdī of Baṣrah (d. 786). Nāzik gave an example of what she meant in a poem titled "The Cholera" that she wrote on October 27, 1947, thus marking the birth of what she called "free verse" in Arabic. This is obviously a misnomer, as the poet, before everyone else, knew that free verse proper has neither set prosodic measures nor a rhyme scheme of any type. So she was saying the wrong thing for the right reason. The idea was caught up by contemporary poets, especially by Al-Sayyāb, who later claimed that he had written some poems in the same style even before Nāzik had explained her idea. This started a rather insignificant discussion among critics and commentators. The important thing is that the new style of writing poetry was picked up and practiced by other poets of the time, especially Al-Bayyāti and Buland, who took the style several steps further.

In discussing Buland's poetry, some commentators like to dwell on the rather irrelevant fact that the poet was of Kurdish origin and was brought up in the Kurdish area of northeastern Iraq. But I think what is more significant is that he was very keen on developing his language of Arabic culture, especially poetry, even though he did not finish school and obviously never had a university education. But his genuine desire to educate himself with whatever sources of knowledge were available made him a sort of *Philosophus autodidactus*. He could not read any European language, but he became an avid reader of translated books from any European language, thus becoming rather knowledgeable of the modern European schools of literature and philosophy. His poems reverberate with the names and ideas of German and French authors, especially French surrealists.

I have known the poet very well from the early 1970s, and we met on several family and social occasions with some of the intellectuals of the time. I have never heard him speaking, let alone celebrating, the fact of his family origins or his Kurdish connections. But in his later days, when he was squarely asked about his Kurdish origins, he did not deny them, nor did he enlarge on such an insignificant point when discussing his poetry and cultural background.

Buland started writing poetry in the mid-1940s and published his early poems in the prestigious Egyptian magazine *Al-Kātib*. Like several of his contemporaries, he was an admirer of the Arab poets of the time, Egyptians, Lebanese, and Syrians. This shows in his first collection of poetry, *Clay Throb* (1946), which was probably known in 1945. This means that the poet was barely twenty years old, which explains his attraction to the published Arabic poetry of the time, which was not uncontaminated by the French fin de siècle aspects of literature, especially poetry.

Buland's second collection, *Songs of the Dead City* (1951), shows a marked growth out of his youthful romanticism, generally borrowed from the Arab poets who were at the core of the poetic education of his generation. The poems of this collection may suggest a kind of "pessimism" on the part of the poet. But the fact is that he found himself at odds with his society, of which he was a part. As he could not do much to set things right in that society, for reasons mainly social, but also political, the poet turned inside and started describing what he considered wrong, and rather vicious, in the society he knew very closely. A poem like "Postman" is a bitter explanation of the seclusion of poets in society: we are far away from the world, and there is nothing new to us. As the poet realized that dreaming of the pleasant past did not take him anywhere, he felt that a revolt against the society might set things right. Little by little, we find Buland, like other intellectuals of his generation, tending more and more to the socialist left, though he was never a member of any political party. But the expression of those sentiments in poetry and in the work of contemporary writers incited the authorities of the country, under different regimes, against Buland and some of his contemporary "rebels," which led them to leave home and start a journey of exile in other countries. Buland's exile was never, really, as unpleasant as it may seem at first. The party that came to power in Iraq in 1963 was not the party of change for the better, the poet felt. So, he exiled himself to Beirut, where he found many friends and poetry lovers who made his stay both pleasant and productive. Coming back to Baghdad in 1971, he was well received by intellectuals, but felt he could not stay more than twelve years, so he exiled himself to London and proved himself there even more productive in poetry and art criticism than before.

It was in Beirut in 1972 that Buland received well-rounded recognition of his poetic achievement. His poem "Dialogue in Three Dimensions" was hailed the best poem of the year. It was in early 1971, as far as I can remember, that Buland came to visit me in our house at the University Quarters in Baghdad and handed me a manuscript of that poem, asking me to translate it into English, as he hoped to find a publisher for it. I translated the poem the week after and gave him a copy, keeping a carbon copy for myself. I still have that translation, which I thought I should include now, as the poem appeared as the last one in Buland's collected works of 1974. The poem shows a significant development in style, not only in the use of the dramatic treatment but also in the multi-faceted suggestions of the symbolism in the poem.

I have added to the complete works of 1974 some poems that were published in magazines and newspapers after that date, which I thought should be included in this book, the last of which dates from about a month before his departure. These eighty poems may give a good picture of the poet's development of style and also a picture of the literary and poetic atmosphere in Baghdad and Iraq from the mid-1940s to the close of the twentieth century.

A NOTE ABOUT THE TRANSLATION
OF ARABIC POETRY

As I have done in several of my previous books of selected poems that
I translated into English, I find it necessary to explain to the non-Arabic
reader some of the points of Arabic grammar and syntax that have no
equivalents in English and some other European languages. This makes
the translation, if accuracy is to be secured, a bit unusual to the Euro-
pean reader, in this case the English-language reader. First, Arabic is so
rich in synonyms for which no two names of one object could mean
the same thing when used because of the nuances and shades of mean-
ing that go with each name of an object. To fail to provide the shades of
meaning in the English word chosen affects the meaning and connota-
tion of the sentence or phrase where that word occurs. Second, verbs in
Arabic decline in the singular, dual, and plural, and the declension of
each verb is affected by the masculine and feminine, an aspect of Ara-
bic that is not found in English or French or any of the Latin-derived
European languages. Moreover, the rhetorical devices used in Arabic
cannot find a happy equivalence in English or other European languages.
Also, Arabic poetry, classical and modern, has a profusion of symbols
of a historical and cultural nature. This demands the use of a great num-
ber of footnotes, which may be heavy on the reader when it becomes nec-
essary to read a footnote and then go back to the text. A sentence that be-
gins with a verb is more expressive and more poetic than a sentence that
begins with a noun or pronoun. When we realize that nouns, pronouns,

adjectives, and verbs must respect the conjugation and declension with the masculine, feminine, dual, and plural, the difficulty of translation and reception by the non-Arabic reader becomes daunting to both. Despite all these "predicaments" the poetry lover should not be discouraged.

Cambridge, United Kingdom, December 2020
'Abdulwāḥid Lu'lu'a

From *Clay Throb*
(1946)

خفقة الطين

1. SEMIRAMIS

The night is drunk
With the tipsy fire.
The darkness outlines shivered.
A breeze ran,
A curtain fluttered,
And he was ravished by the lowering laugh.
So he slipped from a room,
And a bed that was lying in her benumbed heart.
He saw the night a candle,
Vanishing,
In the tears, wallowing in light,
Releasing its melancholy light, dozing
Dozing in the bed.
A whisper lighted on the silent ear,
And waged fire
In the fluffy bed.
The silent baby girl gathered the hopes
And recoiled to her enchanted cave.
The day clamor dozed.
So what has moved
The feeling in the intoxicated night?
A passion?
Depression days are gone,
And folded
Was the bed of frantic love.
A secret penetrated in yesterday's tale,
Which woke up death
In the Assyrian heights.
The Palace emptied
Except for a void,
Stormed by destruction agony.
The Palace emptied
Except for a beauty
That was worshipping silence,

In the large void.
The desire for blood withered out,
So ran mad
The clay worm in the captured blood.
Where is Ninus Her desired husband?
Where are the delights of his memorable past?
Every vein in her body
Is writhing
With the clamor of her heated suffocation.
Her fine yesterday has dozed and is gone
In the wilderness:
A heap of fragrance.
The hall has become an absence and stupor,
Holding what holds her help-seeking heart.
Everything here
Is simply a thing,
A stillness fettered by ages.
How much the night has seen
Of stretching tears
Like wounds on her chilly face!
How dropped the whimper on its tears,
With the throbbing of her poor heart!
How often she has wished
She could be a shepherd's daughter,
Burning the night by the bread-oven light!
How often she had wished
She could be part of a dream
Not fettered to a wicked world,
Not soiled by deep clay once,
Whose echo was not aged among palaces.
How often she has wished
If those pearls
On her chest, as false witness,
Were sighs crystallized.
The world drawn by love
From a conceited blood,

Or hopes of a passionate lover,
Or tears of a conceited poet!
What good is her crown?
Can it nourish the avid body
With its glaring light?
What good is her lofty throne,
Singing for its victorious age?
In her crown there is no life-madness.
In her throne there is no feeling-shine.
On the bed she writhes,
Hoping to plant feeling in the treacherous bed.
This is how autumn dusted the eyeballs
That were still a home for light.
This is how darkness joined her glare
On the way down to bitter loss.

* * *

Semiramis, that is what I know about your heart.
Semiramis, who is that dozing by your side?

* * *

Silence was bored one night,
And stretched
In the deep stillness,
A whiff of a robe
Crossing the hall like an image.
Tender,
Avoiding the times of noise.
On the bank of darkness
Appeared
Two throbs of glaring light
In which the heart reflected
Of its blood
Some shades of reckless desire
Over their light,
A turn of years and a tremor of a thought,

Red. What secret
Is in her eyes clamor?
What secret is in these echoes?
Now wait,
A door moved,
A ray in the black loophole.
On the lips of stillness
Dozed some tears of dumb revolt,
Discharged from the body altar
By the sins, and were lost in the void
With visions,
Creating feeling in the dark,
Softening the shades with allurement.
Oh Āshūr,
There is your crown lying,
Writhing on the semen of desire.
There is Ramesis,
A worm coveting
The earth carrion,
The meteors' revolt.
She choked on poisons, until diminished
The images of purity in reckless visions.
She burned her soul
And memories of nights.
How perfumed they were
By loyalty tremors!
On the throbbing bed rained blizzards
Over two clods of desire.
She hugged her son, and flowed her blood
From the echo of her near, far past.
She hugged him,
Hugging memories,
Stumbling in the blood madness.
Here, here is a young spring
And an autumn tendered with winter.
Vice stormed them both,

So dwindled
The trick of purity and insincere chastity.
A shout:
Ninas . . . that is your mother,
So get drunk
On the nectar of blind sin.
Sully the abusive past,
And crash under your feet
The holiness of children.
You, what are you
But a heap of clay
Holding what things holds the soil.
Hey, what?
In your eyes I see my soul,
My madness,
And the storms of my call,
And a hell
Peeping from the eye hole,
Creeping in the dumb hall.
Hey, what?
I see you fear winds
Whose harm I stirred by my blood.
Why do you feel life in the procession of fire
And let my whims shoot back from my blood?
Answer the call of ribaldry!
A call answered,
And the season slipped into the hidden conscience.
The night turned its neck
And woke up
On the lips of life, the spirit of light.
Then it dozed
In the palace deep hole, like a dream
And remained a white whisper,
And saw . . . a story,
Then arose a question
In the veins of soft stillness.

* * *

Semiramis, who is the one dozing by your side,
Pouring vice in your heart?

* * *

It is my son, oh night, who is born of your terror.

2. AUTUMN ECHO

A heart, leaning on memory crutch,
Went looking in the remains
Of what has gone by,
For an image forgotten in my days' vault.
Oh heart,
Let alone the past
And its remains.
The year's hand has defaced all its glamor.
You shall not see
But my phantoms and illusions,
Where I kept dancing them with lies
For days
Until, with time, they turned
Into tunes.
With their delusion I refresh
The thirsty heart of youth.
If you were looking
For my love,
For my hope,
Love has dozed.
The whisper of kisses died,
After despair wine
Filled my cup.
Or if you were asking about my handsome dreams,
Those are a heap of illusions
That drowned my dawn
One day
And left nothing but your bloodied despair,
As I have forgotten youth. . . .
Leave it to the world,
You will not restore everything to me
By remembering it,
Except inciting my sorrows
And pains.

Enough pain,
It is what is in today's cups,
And love writhing in the hand of nothingness,
Perplexed,
Where shrunk was my dreams' fountain.
I see that you insist on forgetting its image.
My love is nothing but my dreams and suffering,
Which bore my years' burdens.
Today they dozed behind the unknown
Weakened, as if they were bored
By a promise without hope,
Fluttering on bloodied chord and tunes.
Likewise, let your world days sleep,
As misfortune is dancing on my way and yours:
"The turn of the year may kill you a thousand times."

3. WHIMPER

It slept on my dozing eyelids,
Spreading among silence my sorrows.
I melted it
From a heart blood,
Melted in a wave of my sorrow fire.
I squeezed it from a failing hope,
Like a rose crushed under my feet.
Even the one I watered
By a shower of my heart blood
Uncovered my secrets.

* * *

Oh, my tear,
Night phantoms have darkened
In my shabby room.
For God's sake
Leave me to my loneliness
To reveal to the candle my sorrows.
My candle is a poet
Who has sung me light in my atmosphere.
She complained to me about fire,
And I complained to her
About a fire of love in my throbbing heart,
Fighting the night of no end
As if darkness is my days.
Yellow in color, like the image
Of the one I offered my lifetime and dreams.
O, my candle, are you sick,
Or have my ailments run into you?
Or is that paleness in her face
A reminder inflaming my desires?
O, my candle,
The days of love are gone,

I buried them in my illusions' night.
Nothing but my love is left
Except a muddled echo
Deploring my hopes.

4. DREAMING SILENCE

Enough suffering,
Calm down.
Time is tired and cannot feel.
In vain you desire the morning.
Your morning's death
Was announced,
Your eyes
Are pale in the horrible waves of darkness,
Looking for storms,
Black, not abating.
Two dreams
Escaping from the distant tragic past
Landed painfully with their grief.
Lie
On my chest, rest your drunk body
And calm down.
Let your vivid hair braids
Kiss my tears.
We have shot out of the earth's orbit,
So, smile with me!
Why do I see you
As a poet
Kneeling on the road dream,
Blind, on crutches of fears and suspicions
Without a companion;
Creeping on youthful dawn,
Stumbling on morning steps,
Thinking the light is a white doze
In the deep valley.
His hesitating dreams will end
In an ancient eternity.
There is nothing but people,
Worms that sleep and wake.

Nothing but the earth,
Our impudent throbbing,
Nothing but our traces
Vanishing in the road memory.

5. BOREDOM

O, phantoms of extinction,
Here is my life, destroy it.
I am bored with life.
Change light into darkness,
Step with your feet
On my wearied lifetime.
I am bored with a life of silence ruins
And tears,
Weaving misery around me,
Heaping dropping cares
On my heart,
Pulling it down with fatigue.

* * *

We had enough of time,
We drank enough of years,
So, extinction, pull down the curtain
And tear yesterday's reader,
Love and the play.

* * *

When, yesterday, I cried
Her palm would kindly caress my eyelids.
How by her lips she stirred my tears
To refresh her heart from mine.

* * *

How on dreamy shores we reveled,
Singing of marvelous hopes.
Then I saw life as visions of love,
Dreaming, in a sky of eyes.

* * *

When time folded my horizon,
She opened a time
For me between her eyes,
And from her eyes she poured a sky
Where, drunk, I moved about.

* * *

Where has that morning gone?
Nothing of it is left
But a memory that to my heart adds grief
And whimper,
Wrapped in remains of a heart
Melting and perishing in despair.

* * *

Oh, phantoms of extinction,
Pass quickly,
I have known life in every turn.
I knew that calm lives in death,
And the falls of hope
Are the limits of the grave.

6. CLAY THROB

Sins have seeped in my lifetime!
So dance, elated
Over my broken heart.
Grief has chewed my youth, when young,
So chew with ultimate lust my destiny.
I do not crave God's paradise,
Nor do I long for it in my feelings,
Neither do I fear eternal hell.
How often has my Time cast me in my hell!
I am of fire,
My fire is lust
That burnt my body
And sailed in my conscience.
We are, who are we but humans,
Born of the base clay throb?
Our mother, Eve, a blatant sin,
Her past is still a brothel of evils.
Her serpent dance that she sang
Is still shrieking in every chest.
It is still a way to the world tragedy,
An echo to better sorrow irony.
So quit the assumption that you raised
A holy idol
In the naïve assumption altar.
There is no noble or ignoble
On the Time stage.
We are all images of ages.
What we worship today as pure
Will ridicule yesterday's purity.
Between your two darting breasts
Is a promise of a volcano
Of fire and light,
Of all the paradise in our earth.
So violate the grand secret holiness.

Images of sin in your eyes are writhing
Like snakes writhing in hell.
Release them to feed on my blood,
And set them up as a Sodom in my bed.
There are still in the body mud
Some remains of a drunk
Like the worms of a grave.
Sin, in their dreams,
Is singing of blaze, evil, and exciting night.

7. SHADES

From which valley,
Deep-bottomed like a dream
You came, carrying in your eyes
The voice of my blood?
I have forgotten love
And the past.
Lifetime fingers jumped
To raise the repentance tale.
O, her image!
Your world has left nothing of my body,
So what can I give the worms of my remains?

* * *

You allured me by red nights,
So on their black lips my banners slipped.
My past was, across evil, lost,
And left nothing for my future
Except violent echo
And some images
That fell like shades
In the darkness of my evenings and nights.

8. CLOSED LIPS

Oh, how many a world
In my bloodied silence die!
How many hopes
On the illusion path were wearied by silence.
How many lips
In my blood were hushed
By hateful despair!
So what?
They were all gone, but a spider remains,
Weaving death for my silence,
And like me, it will die.

* * *

O, you, hiding in a corner, like my life,
Wrapped in a silly colored shade,
Looking like my hopes,
Where my days' solitude
Cast some of my self;
In your deserted temple
I have sanctified my liberty.
If you are weaving death for me,
Then, like me, you shall die.

From *Songs of the Dead City*
(1951)

أغاني المدينة الميتة

9. BARRENNESS

The same road,
The same houses bound by deep effort.
The same silence.
We used to say:
Tomorrow it will die, and will rise,
In every house
Sounds of small children,
Rolling, with the day, on the road.
They will deride our past,
Our grumbling women,
Our frozen eyes, without luster.
They will not realize memories.
They will not understand the ancient road.
They will laugh, because they are not asked
Why they laugh.

* * *

We used to say:
Tomorrow we shall realize what we say.
The season will bring us together.
Here's a friend,
There is a bashful friend,
Yesterday there was a strong passion.
Perhaps
We did not mean what we used to say.
Today seasons bring us together.
That friend — has no friend.
That passion — is an insolent face.
And on the road,
The same road,
The same houses bound by deep effort.
The same silence,
And there,
Behind the closed windows,

Were sunk eyes,
To wait for children,
Fearing that the day will pass
With the road.

10. DEPTHS

Do not fear
This wind, which is driven from door to door,
All that horizon, growing,
With terror and confusion,
And the roads.
They are the playground of my youth dreams,
They are part of me,
They twist like a serpent,
But do not fear.
They are part of me,
They are my depths,
Which do not know what is with me.
They are my joy whistling in my desolate waste.
Here,
How often the child built his hopes
As sand and hills of dust.
Here,
How often I have come
When the past was a green youth,
And I sang your eyes,
My youth.
Do not fear,
I am but this wind,
Driven from door to door.
I am but that horizon,
Growing in fear and confusion.

11. POSTMAN

Postman,
What do you want?
We are far away from this world,
You made a mistake
No doubt, as there is nothing new
That the world has for this fugitive.
What has been,
Is still the same,
Dreaming,
Or buried,
Or retrieving.
People still have their feasts,
And a funeral memorial,
Joining one feast to another.
Their eyes dig up from their memory
For another bone to feed new hunger.
China still has its wall,
An effaced myth,
And a repeating age.
The Earth still has its Sisyphus,
And a rock,
Which knows not what it wants.

* * *

Postman,
You are mistaken
No doubt, as there is nothing new.
So go back on your way,
Since your way brought you here,
What do you want?

12. IMAGE

The Palace,
By the turn of the town,
Is blocked on both sides by sad visions,
Where can shout in silence
Its dark, cursed desolation.

* * *

It can almost shout: How cruel
Is this glare, drowned in its whisper.
Tomorrow,
When hand folds up its world,
It will remain as I see it,
Stretching in a horrible smile,
Stretching in its dubious yellowness,
Holding history in a stupor,
With which the body has sanctified its sins.

* * *

This glare, sneaking in silence,
Like a whisper of suspicions,
What is behind it?
What mad blaze
Lies in the dust-faced bed?

* * *

Calling to man:
What is man?
What is the soul?
What is God?
What is faith?
Gleams that have no color.
They will vanish,
And the fires survive.

* * *

In the fire,
In the great relief,
From the cruelty of soul, and conscience,
When man calls: What is my destiny
Except the passion blazing in my roots,
Except the passion pulsing in my veins,
Leading me like the free levity,
Blind, without dream,
Without road?

* * *

Except passion,
An atmosphere is well violated.
Except passion,
And Eve was let down.

* * *

Eve,
Of the wicked eyes,
Like deserted mines,
How time with her has wallowed its ages,
And she remained, as in the past,
Filth.

* * *

A filth of vicious visions,
Since God gave her eternal life,
He gave her a poisonous hope,
So she eternalized
His old slip,
And we are still orbiting in her eyelids,
Requesting death
At her hands.
O eternity sinking in her eyes,
How eternal is death here, by her.

* * *

How eternal is death. . . .
And here is Āshūr,
Eyelids choked by feelings,
Crucified by this imprisoned light
In the aperture of the Palace,
Which is sinking,
Sinking in the turn of the town,
With both sides blocked by sad visions,
Whose dark cursed desolation
Could almost shout, in the silence.

13. THREE SIGNS

And we met,
It was a cold amity between our hands.
There was something laughable in our eyes.
I said in whisper:
—You have changed.
—And you.
I turned to myself
And felt pain for my past.
Did it wrong us?
Did we?
Were we misled by our steps
And were ended?
Some sad thoughts,
Some grudge and rancor,
And symbols of a city
That were not raised by our villages.
Did we?
Were we misled by our steps, and met
On roads not taken by our youth,
And we separated?
We separated,
And met.
There was a feeling, not ours, in our hands.
There was something painful in our life.
There was a silence,
And a faraway speech behind our silence.
The world had a lifetime,
And limits.
I said in a whisper,
To myself:
—These are not our villages,
These are not our worlds.
They do not know my past.
With my voice,

I felt my desolation,
My degraded death.
Did we,
Where we misled by our steps,
And met,
And parted,
And separated,
Then we came back and met?
There was a silence between us, deriding us.
There was a dead amity between our hands.
We did not say that we,
But we were,
Finished,
And departed.
I do not rem . . .
We do not remember that we have met,
And separated.

14. THE HYPOCRITICAL WOUND

Do not touch my pride
Do not touch that hypocritical wound.
I know,
I know the place of my ailment in my soul,
I know.
So leave me.
Do not say: Why did you not come to me.
Do not say: You have become arrogant.
You know,
And I know,
That we have thus come to an end,
Proudly.
So leave me.
I have nothing but my pride,
That hypocritical wound,
That death which ridicules
Even my end.
So leave me.
Do not say:
You have become arrogant.
You know,
And I know,
That we have thus come to an end, proudly.
Tomorrow
I shall meet you on my way,
As if we have never met.
This way we have come to an end,
Proudly,
So, leave me.

15. AT NIGHT

At night,
When the nights bury their dead,
And tired souls lean on eternity,
The night does not know that my hand
Had woven their tragedies,
From all that they had
And that in the silence of the night
I am downcast,
A feeling within me, astounded, like reason
Calls: O Lord, why did they exist?
Why did the earth have history and times?
Why does this fetter
Eternalize its past,
So people would dream
If you could be alerted by a devil
To see the earth, in all its extents,
With worms swarming her white eyes,
So you do not feel sorry
For what she suffers,
Isn't there a human in your Lordly heart?
Disappointment
Blackened the lofty forehead,
As if a blizzard touched its domains,
Roaring and charging.
A power crumbled,
But people came back, as they used to be,
Their feet tied to the earth
By a serpent,
And the earth is silently weaving her tragedies
From everything she has.

16. HERE YOU ARE

Yesterday, when we were small,
How small the world was!
I still remember those years,
Those dark roads,
The laughter of the drunk,
Returning from life
Without life.
The color of the sky
Like disease, creeping in our blind alleys.
I still remember all those years,
Those round faces,
Dying behind small apertures,
Blind, made of clay and straw.

* * *

How small is the world in our poor district!
Do you remember
Those long stories about the Princess
Who used to insist,
Insist to remain, like our world, small?
I still remember all those years,
The evening color,
My house, frightening like a pest,
The depth of eyes, smiling without hope.
And there, a bitter woman,
A pain we tried to stir.
Then she returns to say:
—No, I am not a bitter woman.
Then she returns to repeat
A tale that kept on longer
Growing, but the Princess does not grow.
That Princess, where is she?
Do you remember?
How small the world was,
And today how big it became, eh?
—No, I'm not a bitter woman.

17. ROADS

Filling the road,
A deep silence,
Breaking from worry and distress.
And there, on the profound horizon,
Are ways that sleep
And wake.
But I,
I became tired, and here
I shall sleep,
Not moving, and no hopes move.

* * *

Without promises,
Without pledges,
And let those ways
Remain on the remote horizon,
As they wish.
Tomorrow they will dally again.
But I,
I have become tired,
And here, I shall sleep,
Not moving, and no hopes move.

18. OLD AGE

Another winter,
And here I am,
Next to the heater,
Dreaming that a woman may dream of me.
I dream to bury in her chest
A secret,
So she cannot deride her own secret.
I dream to set lights
In my lifetime bent,
Saying:
This light is my own,
So no woman can approach.

* * *

Here,
Next to the heater,
Another winter,
And here I am,
Weaving my dreams and fearing them.
I fear her eyes may deride
A foolish bald on my head,
A white hair in my soul.
I fear her feet may kick
My love,
And I end up there,
Next to the heater,
A toy in the hands of a woman.

* * *

Another winter, and here I am,
Alone,
No love,
No dreams,

No woman
With me.
And tomorrow I shall die of cold,
Here,
Next to the heater.

19. DREAM

You, who are dreaming now,
What are you dreaming?
Of the blue roads,
Of the forest,
Of dying with the world
That you do not understand?
Perhaps I am now a thing,
A forest,
Or the road,
Or the death that you do not understand.
Or maybe I am now
A grip that suffocates you,
An eye that does not wink,
Or a severe winter
That slips into your heart
Every now and then.
And what then?
You who are dreaming now,
What are you dreaming of?
And tomorrow, when you perceive the dawn,
What will you perceive?
You were a dream
That passed with the night,
Of no meaning, like the prison's days.
And you vanished with the road,
With the forest,
And the death that you do not understand.

20. AN OLD LOVE

Do you remember?
And you were ashamed of what you remember.
As for me,
I laughed, laughed at what you remember.
We were young,
Perhaps we did not know how young we were.
Do you remember?
The day was dying on the sad horizon,
As was usual for years.
There was a waiting,
And the train arrived
And shook many hands
Many hands,
Except my hand.
Do you remember, except my hand?
It was prepared for the finest rendezvous.
But you passed,
Passed over and did not turn.
You did not seek my hidden secret,
And you laughed like the others.
But I felt ashamed,
Ashamed of my insulted love.
Do you remember?
And you were ashamed of what you remember.
But I laughed,
Laughed at what you remember.

21. SLAVERY

Slave . . . !
I can almost revolt, but
I feel the fetter in my ear,
Sarcastically howling at me,
And cry laughingly, slave!
Slave! I am my human creator,
I am the demolisher and builder,
I am my Lord and devil.
Do you think, oh fetter?
It sarcastically whispered . . . Slave!
Slave!
I can almost go mad,
Are you, is that you, my sense,
Is this the forgotten world,
Cast by the cradle,
Gathered by the grave?
Is the one crying you, slave?
Slave!
I am the one who lives in my shade.
I, the death without shape.
But who are you, my fetter?
The voice became stronger,
As if storms were bellowing
In me, and vanishing:
I am, you are, I am the slave.

22. O MY FRIEND

O my friend,
Why don't you pick up your past
And get out of my way!
We have finished and ended,
We have remembered so much
And forgotten what we remembered,
Years and years,
We have thrown out of our hands
All we have saved of that deep love,
All we have saved of the remote past:
The visions we had,
All that we had,
We folded, and we returned to be folded.
O my friend,
You no longer know a thing of my friend,
O my friend!
Why don't you pick up your past
And get out of my way!
Why don't you look for a new world!
In the earth there are still happy dreams.
Then what?
What use for you is a remote memory?
We have finished and ended.
We have remembered so much,
And forgotten what we remembered,
Years and years.
Then I lost my enemy from my friend.
O my friend,
Why don't you pick up your past
And get out of my way!

23. DECEIT

Through
The sands thirst for waters,
Life to us looked
Like images of mirage.
So we kept sinking in deviation.
The road looks like what we see.
My thirst is deadly,
The road looks like what we see.
My fatigue is hateful,
The road looks like what we see.
What is behind it?
This turning back to life . . .
What is behind it?
Here you are you,
And not you.
Your world is some night and silence.
This night, what is behind it?
Should we still sink in deviation,
And through the sands thirst for waters?
Should life keep on deceiving us?

24. LOST STEP

The winter was scratching the station platforms.
A storm was mewing like a cat.
And on the road
An old lantern was shaking,
To shake our stingy village.
What shall I do in the city?
You asked me,
What will you do in the city?
Your silly step will be lost
In its large streets.
The blind alleys will crush you
And will grow the night in your deaf depths.
Sad hopes,
What will you do in the . . .
Without a friend?
No . . .
There is no friend in the city.
You laughed at me,
You ridiculed me,
But I remained waiting for the train to the city.
You left me,
And I left you.
But through the train's glass window
Villages passed,
Floating and sinking in the sand,
And I was waiting for the day
At the city.

* * *

Years passed,
Dark nights grew in my eyes
And flared your clouds, O darkness!
To whom shall I return?
To my village?

Or to winter scratching the station platforms?
To the small lanterns, shaking over stingy villages?
Or to the women dead of life?
No . . .
I shall not return,
To whom shall I return,
When my village became a city,
On every turn there is a light,
On every step end
There is light of a new lamp.
It would shout at me:
What do you want? What do you want?
You, wandering shadow,
What do you want?
Nothing knows me here.
Nothing I know here.
Nothing I remember.
And nothing remembers me here.
I shall drag my little step
In its large streets,
And shall crush me, the blind alleys.
No . . .
I shall not return,
To whom shall I return?
My village has become a city,
Has become a city.

25. LOSS

You ran after his visions, but
You lost nothing but his visions.
You looked into his eyes, and found
No one else.
He himself
Is still deriding your passion,
And his passion.
He goes on deriding: what is life?
He himself,
The world still sees him,
And does not see him.
He walks where his steps take him.
—No,
I shall not see him,
This cursed passion,
I shall not see him.

* * *

O his naked death! Here she is like them.
She failed to know his range,
She failed to know his passion,
She is like them, like the others,
like the world,
Sees and does not see him.
And you still say: How cruel is life!
And he still derides: What is life?

26. WHERE TO?

Where to?
Woe! Do not ask.
Like you, my feet are asking.
I sail, with the night, in my hope,
And wake up to find nothing
But Time, turning the nights around my spindle,
As thin threads of smoke colors,
Tomorrow my fingers will spread
As a curtain to hide my degraded weakness.

* * *

Where to?
What an echo, silence!
There is nowhere
Behind by disengagement.
The land shrank before my step,
And was lost
Before two begging eyes.
I am still walking on my forehead,
And behind my steps humiliation sneaks,
As if on dead lips I trample,
Sucking what to me they inspire,
Folding my life on a laughter,
Its creation to be enjoyed
By two desperate souls.

From *Steps in Exile*
(1965)

خُطُوات في الغربة

27. SECRET

I know,
You will return to burn my hair,
You will return
To uproot my nails.
You won't kill me,
You will tighten the rope,
But you won't kill me.
You will trample on my chest,
I know,
And on a mouth that won't let out my secret.
What a secret!
The lash will howl in my flesh,
Like poison.
It will go through my body.
What a secret!
You will dig in my voice agony,
In my death,
In my bitter silence,
You would shout, I want, I want, I want,
And the lash repeats.
You will say, it will suffocate him,
It will burn him.
What cowardice!
Shall I disgrace my son?
No—No.
The shout whoops in my eye:
No—No.

* * *

Then you will return to burn my hair,
To uproot my nails;
But my secret
Will remain like your dagger in my chest,
Two symbols of a free man.

Oh fool!
In my secret is my excuse
To shout,
To spit,
To ridicule a free
Slave.

28. OLD IMAGE

A cup,
A song,
And a dubious woman.
What are you trying to be?
— What are—
What an echo!
As far as my eyes can see,
Sink in silence
Steps of melancholy generations.
And on my hand,
In every black vein
Doze years,
Which passed in vain,
A dream that materialized
As a fireplace in my winter.
In it I burned all my past,
But my future did not warm up.
What am I trying to be?

* * *

And my monotonous pulse sinks.
— What — try —
No —
I should not answer.

* * *

O you,
O dubious woman,
Sing,
Dance,
Clip the wing of a fly so it cannot fly,
And let it creep on the dust to destiny,
And let the large universe
Sneer as it likes.

Let the large universe sneer
At a fly
With a clipped wing,
At a small heart.
For I, like you,
Have, in the past, been taken by the days
From one house to another.
We gave up love,
We gave up hope,
And as I ended, you ended,
Two shadows
Of night and silence.

* * *

O you,
O dubious woman,
Sing,
Dance,
Tell tales of the lost
To the lost.
Add the sins of the others
To others.
For I, like you,
Am left here, with all my death,
A cup, a song,
Some cigarettes and errors of years,
Cast, as melancholy toys,
A dalliance for a dubious woman.

* * *

What am I trying to be?
What — try —
And sink my monotonous pulses
No —
I won't answer.

29. JUDAS'S REPENTANCE

O my children,
I know that my shame
Is a story that flows from one house to another.
I know that
Whenever a winter hugs a fire,
Whenever lips pass by a name,
Like my name,
They remember my sin,
My sin, a dagger goes deep in my children's hearts.
I know that
What my hands have stolen,
What palaces have built,
For my future,
Have become nothing but a witness
To my destruction.
I know that
Whatever I hoarded in the night,
Of destruction,
Of the innocent and the poor,
Of blood I shed to please my evils,
Have turned up today,
In the light,
Witness to my collapse.

* * *

I know that
Rancor is eating my people's veins
Whenever sees me the beast that crushed its rights,
Whenever sees me the night which blocked its way.
I know
Which beast,
Which night,
I was on you, my people.
I know

How I cast you on the way,
Leaving you with
Nothing but hunger,
And destruction.
What use is my apology
After I burned even my neighbor's house?
O my children,
A death sentence will not wipe away my shame
Off my forehead.
Here—
There is a thousand killed,
There—
A thousand prisoned,
And here—
A thousand children who gained nothing
But my prisons.
I know
That a death sentence will not wipe away my shame.
So disavow me, my children
And leave me.
Leave me as a curse
Creeping in history from one fire to another.
Perhaps it will wash off my shame.

30. YOU CAME WITH THE DAWN

You came with the dawn,
And here was
A massacre growing with no excuse.
And behind the prison door,
There were hopes
Living languidly,
And treason had
A thousand hands stealing from my mind,
And from my free blood,
The black night's desire for the dawn.

* * *

You came with the dawn,
And we were here,
Killed silently, and we did not know.
Can man be crucified,
Can fires burn
Our houses,
Our children,
Because we dream of the dawn?
But you came,
And we were here,
Asking where hopes come from,
Where from?
They will not come,
The sun will not shine,
When in my house
Sink in death,
Silently, my children's feet.
Where from?
It will not come
Since our prison is blind,
With no aperture,
And our road is diving in the abyss,

And we have no power, no might.
But you came, and we were here,
A story about our bitter past,
And a procession of light
In our free dawn.

31. BITTER LAND

Who knows?
We may depart at dawn.
Do not cast
An anchor.
Do not sow
A seed.
The land here is deaf like a rock,
Blind like a rock,
The cliff waters are bitter.
Do not cast
An anchor,
Do not set up
A tent,
We shall die
Before a cloud passes above,
To become life in a rose.

* * *

Do not cast
An anchor.
Do not sow
A seed.
Who knows,
We may depart at dawn
From a land deaf like a rock.

32. I WANT TO

I want to delve in crowded streets,
A tale,
Or a song,
Or an epic,
Stretching my ear to every laugh
And murmur.
I want to understand
What becomes wet in a smiling tear,
To understand
What is in a whoop sobbing like wind
Through broken ribs.
I want to
Ask who
Dreams of—his dreams.
I want to
Ask who suffers.
Sufferers of—his pains,
Of a poisoned drop
In his broken cup.
I want to remove the night
So under its shade
No serpent hides
Or creeps behind its foot,
Spitting out a thousand taboo thoughts.
I want to
Awaken a dark world,
To shake a lamp,
Here, there,
Whose light is full of hopes,
Lighten a height and bent.
I want to be like others,
With an accuser, a plaintiff, and a court;
To have a dawn like theirs,

A night like theirs, planting its stars in me,
To have a road like theirs,
To pass through it,
As a story, a song, or an epic.

33. TOMORROW HERE

Tomorrow,
Here,
In this turn of our land,
History will ask about me,
Myself.
About that section of our age,
About rooms that were not touched by light.
But we
Were,
And light was
In us,
Flowing from our nights' silence,
From the ring of the fetters on our hands,
From the limits of walls covering us,
Pulling me,
Distancing me,
From a story told — by my son,
From a flower withering in my house,
And eyes frightened by my death,
From a hand
Like my hand, skinny, drawing in silence
Two arms stretching
To tomorrow's dawn.

* * *

Tomorrow,
Here,
History will ask about me,
Myself,
About our house, sunk in darkness,
Our road, desolate like a curse,
About a sigh
Plunging in a smile,
About feet running,

About a nation,
Melting,
Covered by roads,
Barefooted,
Of severed hands,
With nothing in her eyes
Except the extinguished-eyed future.
And you, tale of sins,
Tomorrow, here,
The age will curse you.
And at the top,
History will write about me,
Myself,
About a verdure
Brought in by a cloud.

34. AND TOMORROW I RETURN

In my land
Silence is, like hatred, bitter.
Dawn comes without glitter.
Night passes
And does not go.
People mumble in my land.
We were
Two,
Two eyes diving in two eyes,
Waiting
For the silver dawn.
And dawn comes without glitter
In my land.

* * *

We were bored by running with dreams.
We hated people,
We lost feeling,
Bored,
We died.
And if we lived,
It was for a drop of wine in a cup,
To make us forget
Our nights' darkness,
Forget
A jailer,
And jailed,
And sad memories in the land of cactus.

* * *

We were
Two,
Two eyes passing by two eyes
Without love,

Without hate,
And like some people, we pass by some.
And people
Mumble in my land.
In my house
We were two,
And silently,
Two palms met two palms.
—Are you going?
—I shan't stay—I shan't stay.
And you whispered in a wet voice:
—I shall stay to suffer—I shan't go
By my love,
By my hatred.
I shall turn my fields
Into a dawn, flowing on my land.

* * *

Today
I return.
My land stretches without limits,
My house is a height,
Its two shoulders are roses,
Its world is eternity.
My road,
It is like a conversation of two about love,
About our hearts' desire,
About a generous gesture.
Promises flourish on its sides,
And silently,
Two palms met two palms,
Two eyes dived in two eyes.
In a wet voice you whispered:
Close your eyelids,
To drown in the silver dawn.
How deep,

How pleasant,
How wide — is my land!
That which is larger than my love,
That which is larger than all years of exile,
Of darkness,
Of terror,
And larger than your forgiveness,
O my hatred!

35. HE SAID SOMETHING TO US

Yesterday
He passed by this way.
He said something to us,
And passed by, this way.
Then flowed in our village
A dawn,
And hopes flourished,
Our vines woke up
To bow,
As love,
Shade,
And harvest.

* * *

Yesterday
He passed by this way.
He said something to us,
And passed by this way.
A promise was in his look,
A thunder was in his smile,
And in his hold
A wound and pains that cast a glare
On the land,
On history,
On the world — on us.

* * *

Yesterday
He passed by this way.
He said something to us
And passed by this way.
On his feet
Were his fetters,
In his eyes

Was his struggle,
In his heart
Were his hopes.
His gain was for the people,
And the world, a harvest.

* * *

Tomorrow,
When children frolic in our village,
Tomorrow,
When lights shine from our houses,
A thousand hands,
A thousand mouths,
Will raise, from our life, a salute
To a passer-by,
Who yesterday
Passed this way,
Leaving us something, and passed by
This way.

36. RETURN TO HIROSHIMA

Should I go home?
To whom?
To a dead child,
To a heap of rocks turned into ruins,
Sobbing in silence?
To a baby girl,
Yesterday, here, with her I realized the world
As a waking jasmine flower,
A shake of a plait.
As a bee,
Nahla's two eyes were roaming,
And today,
There,
With the ruins,
There,
With the naked nothingness,
With the silence,
How deep is the valleys' night!
Should I go home,
Should I return to search for my daughter
In a heap of stones,
In a thicket of fire and smoke?

* * *

In a thicket of fire and smoke,
What is the value of a perishing man?
There,
Here,
In a thousand places
Two lips of a man will pray
For death.
Two hands will be rich
By death.
What is the value of a perishing man?

What is the value of perishing thousands,
So that one man may be rich?

* * *

Should I return to my home?
To a dead child?
Should I return to search for a jasmine flower?
For a bee,
For a baby girl,
In the congestion of walking feet?
They will not stop
So that someone will ask
About the agony of a man.
What value
Is the agony
Of a man?

* * *

Should I return to search for my death,
When death is here,
And death is there?
So keep silent.
It will come to you
And from a thousand places.

37. IN A FEW HOURS

They broadcast:
In a few hours
Light will dry in some eyes,
An arm will be paralyzed.
It was rumored
That he was hungry,
So his bitter voice was harbored by the hungry.
Lost he was.
So his lost feet were guided by the hungry.
Criminal he was,
In his look meet
A road, a dawn, and riffraff.
An arm,
A sail,
Crossing history as love,
A call,
A grant,
A ray.

* * *

In a few hours my arm will be paralyzed,
A hand, from behind the prison gate,
Will wave farewell.
A yellow hand, like falsehood, tries to pull me,
But I shall remain
The cry of man everywhere.
I shall remain
An image in every eye,
In every heart.
I shall remain
An idea creeping in silence.
And of my death
Will remain

For the rising tomorrow,
For the dawn,
An arm, an arm, and an arm,
And will glide a sail, a sail, and a sail.

38. A TALK FOR NEXT SATURDAY

In the room,
The same room,
Saturday will pass.
With yearning
She may remember me,
She may ask about me.
—He has not come.
—He will not come.
And silence will sink, in the room.
—Are you crying?
No, no, but I,
I don't know
Why I feel that Saturday is sad,
Why I feel that the house is sad.
I feel that
I am burying something of me
In my silence.
Anxiously,
You may hear my voice,
The sad tone may return to my voice.
Who knows?
You may hear nothing but the steps of death,
Passing through the room,
And disappear without love or yearning.
Who knows?
You may mock my voice,
And me . . .

* * *

And all the widowed hours in my secret.
—He has not come.
—I hope he will not come back.
Others will laugh in the room.

* * *

In the room, the same room,
Saturday will pass,
You may remember me.
You may ask about me.
May — no,
What use is that — I am dead,
Dead in the room, the same room.

39. THE EIGHTH JOURNEY

Turn off your lanterns, let us drown
O guard of the lighthouse.
The dream in your blue maze
Has wearied the mariner.
He wished it could end,
That tale of the seas,
That touring in the seas,
That tale of pearls, corals, and shells.
He wished he could drown.

* * *

Turn off the lights for him,
Turn off, and do not worry.
Leave him to the current,
Carrying to the depths
What depths has the dream,
Carrying to the pearls, corals, and shells
All the tales about aridity
In a world living without heart,
About a sinner
Looking in repentance for a sin.

* * *

O guard of the lighthouse
Leave him to the current
Carrying to the depths what depths he carries
In his hands, in his eyes,
Carrying to the seas,
To their closed waste,
The bitterness of loss in the seas,
The bitterness of cactus,
So leave him.
You should not worry.

40. AT FORTY

At forty,
On my hands are
Loads of hopes that die with no future.
No—
Keep away.
Do not look in my eyes for a rendezvous.
I, for years,
If you know, have become nothing
But an echo of my fugitive steps,
Sliding me
Into a thousand grievous paths.
No—
Keep away,
You—who dream
Of the dawn, born of the dreams
Of fresh flowers,
Of Jasmine.
I, for years,
If you know, have awakened in the thorns
Of my degrading thirst,
My dormant rancor,
The rancor of dead hopes,
On a dark road.
No—keep away,
You, who dream
Of the dawn,
Of the fresh flowers,
Of the Jasmine,
I am, for years, if you know,
Forests of rancor, sleeping for a rendezvous
That may not arrive with tomorrow.

41. TO MY TOWN

They say:
Our house is gloomy.
They say:
Our road
Has lost its freshness by sins.
They say:
People in my town
Had the flame dried in their eyes.
They say,
How wretched is what they say!
Our house is gloomy,
Shades croak in its desolation
And our road is strange.
Its tawny look was deserted by children.
They say,
How wretched is what they say!
That there are no men in my town.

* * *

I know, O my small town,
O sweating men at noon,
O piece of bread on a straw mat,
O little girl weaving a braid in her dreams,
For the story of prince to the princess,
I know, O my town,
How many rich, bitter wounds
Bleed under broken wings.
But I know, O my town,
I know what is behind our gloomy house,
What is behind its awesome silence,
What future is gleaming on the roads,
And I
Know, O my town,
I know that in my town men's eyes

Do not wink,
That their silence
Is full of boiling furnaces.
Tomorrow,
When they burst,
To them will bow tomorrow.

42. STEPS IN EXILE

This is me,
Cast, there are two bags,
And steps exploring on a pavement
That leads nowhere.
From a thousand ports I came,
And to a thousand ports I may be sent.
In my eyes lie a thousand expectations
No, I was not finished.
No—not finished.
Laden are your vines, O road,
Thirsty are still the casks,
And I fear,
I fear my silent, sad nights may wake
To see life
As what tells us life:
A waving hand in a pavement
That leads nowhere.

* * *

No—
I am not finished,
As behind all the nights of this earth,
I have a love and a house.
A love and a house will remain
Despite all their anxious and agonizing stillness.
Despite what rancor and hatred holds the wound.
There will still be for me
Love and the house,
And Time may bring me back.

* * *

If it did,
If my eyelashes could hold
My blue sky–serenity,

Would a heart in that house
Throb for me?
Would a love remember
The son of that yesterday?
Would two eyes smile
Or ridicule and ask:
— Are you not finished?
What do you want?
Why did you come?
A tale of a thousand dead
I see in your eyes,
They will shout:
Do not come near him.
On his hands, tomorrow,
The morning will commit suicide
And there will be neither road nor splendor.
No —
Chase him out,
For his step holds no cloud
To refresh hopes,
Then they will pass away.

* * *

That is me,
Cast, there, two bags
And life
Is what it says to us:
A waving hand on a pavement,
That leads nowhere.

From *The Journey of Yellow Letters*
(1968)

رحلة الحروف الصُفر

43. *TO A NEGRO FROM ALABAMA*

Say — No,
And spread your wings for us a shade,
Say — No, and bury a dead one,
Build a house,
Cleanse a sister from a black shame,
And learn who you are,
A black god!
Say — No,
And spread your wings for us a shade,
A prayer-place,
For on the way there are a thousand dead,
Still asking for a candle,
For a tear,
For a black god,
Deserted in silence, not worshipped.
O my Lord,
O my sin, sighing in kneeling,
Tell me — No.
We shan't allow,
To be slaughtered.
We shan't allow
You to win a slipper from my skin.
Say — No,
And make from your rancor an arrow for me,
An asp,
Fidgeting between a pregnant woman's breasts,
Spitting pus and poison.
O black god . . . say NO.
My death will not be bread,
But — salt,
Which will sizzle your wounds,
One after another.
Say — No.
Black god,

O black Negro,
Be poison,
Be pus,
Be an eagle,
So you can be worshipped.

44. DISAPPOINTMENTS OF THE MAN OF THE PAST

"The generation of Buland could hardly step out of its first exile
when it found itself in a new exile, though this was,
in its emotional effect, of a deeper and wider nature."

From a critical study by an unknown author

I prayed, sister.
I prayed until sins in my wastes
Became a prayer.
I fasted until my lips dried,
And said: In the lips,
In the wood prepared for winter: I have a God,
And that I am a cloud,
Gifted by His hands,
That I am the dark sand dream of water,
That from my dryness I blow life.
But life was nailing the cross on foreheads,
And crucifying Christ every hour,
Crucifying this dead one every moment,
And my pain reaches its limits,
And in my dry eyes soars the sky.
A story about an errant one, choked by his steps.
And I was, sister,
Carrying loss in my depths.
I prayed,
I fasted,
In my maze I became a god,
And sins in my wastes became a prayer,
My lips dried,
And here I am dying, sister,
Like a god dying in his exile.
And I am nothing but a step
I planted in the sand,
To dream of water.

45. DESOLATION

(1)

—It rings—rings.

—Who are you?

—I am you.

—You make a mistake.

—And the receiver dies in my hand.

(2)

—The sound rings.

—It rings . . . rings . . . rings.

—Who are you?

—I am you.

—You made a mistake, we are two,

From two lands with no colors.

I don't know who you are,

You made a mistake.

. . . and the silence dries,

And death was writhing in the receiver.

Moans . . . moans.

Who are we . . . who are we . . . who are . . .

(3)

The voice rings,

. . . rings-rings-rings-rings.

—Who are you?

—I am you.

—You are mistaken. Mistaken. Mistaken.

—No, you are I,

—And I do not know who we . . .

Are we two,

A generation . . . or two

With time stretching between them?

—I do not know what you mean.

—But . . . I will stay fighting in the receiver,

We'll stay because

I am searching for a voice from me,

Imprisoned in the silence of the receiver,
In the death of the receiver.
(4)
— Mistaken, you are mistaken, mis . . .
. . . and die the two voices with the receiver.
(5)
The sound rings,
Rings, rings, rings, rings, rings.
Generations collapse in my ear.
———— Nothing from you, nor from me.
Who are we . . . who are we. . . .
Two voices die with the receiver.

46. GENESIS

He drowns in her large eyes.
He spreads, in their shades,
Dark as his death, his bed.
On the thousand thoughts lies the prince.
And the princess lies.
Two shadows deserted on an island.
The sun does not rise on my island.
The sun does not set.
The shade does not know how to stretch,
Or shrink,
Or become other than its strange color.
On this island
People are not born,
So in the mirror,
His death will not be his bed.
On a thousand thoughts lies the prince
And lies the princess,
Two shadows deserted on the island.

* * *

The sun does not rise on my island.
The sun does not set.
The shade does not know how to stretch,
Or shrink,
Or become other than its strange color.
On this island
People are not born,
So in the mirror,
There will be nothing except its dubious form,
And he will not see his conscience.

* * *

The island grows,
And grows the sense of time,

And under the weight
Of evening, morning, and noon
The two shadows moved
And came among what came,
Death for man,
And the cursed angry one for the island.

* * *

And it so happened
That the hour turned us in the place
And drowned . . .
Death, man,
On the island.
So there was nothing but the shade at noon,
A shade without man.

47. DREAMING OF RETURN

I dream, O my town, of returning
To our house of extinguished candles.
I dream to return,
To wake up the lamp,
Open the window for the winds,
Leave the key behind the door
For the thieves,
And visitors,
For rendezvous.

* * *

I dream to return, O my town.
I dream of returning
To all the tears in your sore heart,
To your night cast in the alley,
A black sheet, like shame,
Carried by the wonder,
The white slave, the vintner,
From one tavern to another
To laugh in a bar
When hunger and the road may hide,
In its darkness, his torn shoes.

* * *

I dream to return, O my town,
Searching for my eyes in a book
That I left there,
By the door,
So a green reproach grew on its leaves,
"I wish she could return,"
I want to return,
Before they dry in promises
Her questions about a wanderer
In the wind and fog.

* * *

I dream, O my town, of returning
To all the tears in your sore heart.

48. TWO FACES

"One morning, the poet and the Sultan were two faces in my soul."

A fancy of the poet

I will hang your head on the castle gate,
I will gouge out your eyes,
Sever your hands.
For you no tear will drop,
No candle will burn.
I will scatter your flesh in the village
For the hungry of the village,
For the hyenas of the village.
And we shall drink a toast to the free,
For wiping the shame.
The poet is mortal,
But I am the Sultan.
I spread my roots twisting like the slander.
I should wipe out the sorrow of Friday nights,
Believe that,
And wash the village bell
Of every doubt,
Every suspicion,
And every dirt.

* * *

But I,
Believe that I
Felt, as you felt, the shame,
And felt the fire,
And saw the disgrace-man
In the eyes of children
And grown-ups.
And I cried,
As the free cry,

In silence,
And lamented your death in mine.
But
Be assured
That I shall hang your head at the castle
To keep the Sultan spreading
And twisting roots, yellow like slander.

49. MESSAGE OF THE SMALL MAN

"And I hid near our house, which you often talked about
your tears. . . . In this room I was born. . . . At this door of
two shutters my father was killed . . . and . . . who knows!"

From a letter by a liberty-fighter in Yafa

And yesterday, O mother,
I passed by our house,
And I was almost killed near our house.
But I was not afraid.
And I did not shiver,
Your little son, mother,
Because I knew
That death near our house is life.

* * *

Do not laugh.
Be for once
My mother as I want her to be,
Seeing in my eyes the big shadow of my father,
His tender heart,
His resonant voice.
I was no longer, believe me, since I passed by our house,
Your little boy,
Because I knew that death, mother,
I knew that death near our house
Is life.

* * *

Do not cry, mother.
Be for once
My mother as I want her to be,
More than a dreamer,
Afraid that near her house

Her little boy may be killed.
Afraid that he may be crucified in prisons,
Her little boy,
Afraid that I may carry in my eyes
The great shadow of my father.
Afraid that I may become
Bigger than her little boy.

* * *

Do not laugh.
Do not cry, mother.
For yesterday, near our house,
I learned that death
Does not frighten like life.

* * *

I did not fear.
He did not shiver,
Your little boy,
Because I carried in my eyes
The shadow of my great father.

50. THE PALING SALT

The night
May pass, my lady friend,
And the morning may not come.
The land
May flourish, my lady friend,
But there is nothing beside the salt.
And we, as we laugh, my lady friend,
We extinguish every hour
A cigarette in a wound.
But
We do not turn the coffee cup over
And search in its dark lines
For our road
Among the salt deserts
For the morning arrival,
And will not see in the wound
The ashtray of ashes and smoke,
Anything but the burned, degraded blood.
The powerful giant, my lady friend,
Is man,
With all fires blazing in his eyes,
With all desire for the morning the night holds,
With all that throbs behind the wound,
With all that salt holds
Of a call to a cloud,
Crossing in April.
But
We do not turn the coffee cup over,
My lady friend,
Because
We believe that the Earth is for man,
With its night and morning,
With its salt, paling like slander,
With its wound, open for flies and worms.

And because
We believe that our wound
Is deeper than a black drop in a cup,
O my lady friend.

51. AGE OF RUBBER STAMPS

Restore us,
O our age,
O age of rubber stamps,
O harshness of lashes
On our skin,
O fetter for no crime.
Restore to us
Our old eyes,
Our black gloomy doors,
Open to the night and weather.
Restore to us
What shadows shook the candles
In the dark evenings.
Restore to us
Our children, bare under the winter rage,
Where little hands wish
They could tear the sky.
O our age,
O age of rubber stamps,
O fetter for no crime,
O harshness of lashes,
Restore to us
Our old eyes,
To realize the triumph that looms in defeat.
And set up for us
From locust legs in our desert,
From dry cactus in our lands,
From the arms of our dead children,
Gallows,
Asking us
About an anger that carries us,
In a great chant.
We are bored

With your face,
Pinned in rubber,
In soil,
In crime.

52. I WISH IF

I wish if
You were killed, my friend.
I wish if
You were hanged,
You were hung on the road lamp post,
Then I would have said:
That towering thousand banners
Is my friend.

* * *

I wish if
You preferred to be
Larger than your disloyal finger,
Taking it in the darkness of prisons, as a slander,
Hope whatever we deeply notice,
Of arms shouting on the road.
I wish if
You kept silent until death.
O my friend,
Then it would not have been
This, who is selling us . . . my friend.

53. SHORT LAUGH

"In the age of falsehood, the poet says nothing except what is
in his mind, and the reader reads nothing except what is in his mind.
The dialogue continues through short, serious laughs."

From a letter from the poet to a friend

Had we said what we could not understand,
We would have understood from someone
Who did not understand what we said.
We would have become,
In the darkness of dreams,
A vision,
A world that extends and is invoked.
If we said
Death is a sail,
And silence is the bottom,
And people are naked banks,
Mirrored in banks' nakedness,
To twinkle in the eyes of the clairvoyant,
The shell-vendor,
A meaning deeper than silence whispers,
And death terror,
He would have seen in the letters of "said"
A meaning,
That would have had no meaning
Had the fortune-teller not come to us,
Had the fortune-teller not brought us in.

* * *

O land of falsehood,
O age of falsehood,
We should pray to the sea sunk in shells,
To the fortune-teller pebbles,
We shall gouge out the sun's eye

To live in a vision
Of the world that extends and is invoked.
We should pray, O age of falsehood,
To the age of falsehood,
To the fortune-teller falsehood,
For death is a sail
And silence is the bottom
And people are naked shores
Mirrored in shores' nakedness.
The laugh is not to understand
What we understand.

54. THE WAITING SAILS

If you came back, O morning,
You would see me carrying all my faces,
Sails, waiting for the winds,
Waiting for sailing,
To a shore with no pearls or shells.
Nothing,
Except hunger and storms,
And men's feet
Plunging until death in mud,
Plunging behind death and night,
As if they want
To grow from its veins
Roots, branches, and fruits
Wanting to
Shine in full the children's eyes
With a myth
About feet that grow in the mud
In a shore that has neither pearls nor shells,
Nothing but hunger and storms
And the feet of men.

* * *

If you came back, O morning,
You would find me the boat, the sail, the wounds, and the seas.
You would find me shining in full the children's eyes
As if I were
The roots, the branches, and fruits.

55. SUFFOCATION

"When the moment becomes a tale to store years, we would overstep the limits of the man we have known, and the destiny of things in our earth would worry us, and we would look in the space of tomorrow for a corner for ourselves."

From a margin in an old notebook of the poet

Despite the future, open on the horizon,
I feel I'm suffocating,
As if I have swallowed all our land,
Its air,
Its water.
There is nothing in its veins
Except my veins, burning.

* * *

I feel the vomit I have collected
For two thousand years,
From a prostitute's face here
And a saint's face there.
From them
And from my own hunger,
It wraps me, and sets off
To cover houses, faces,
And roads.
While the people are either asking about worries
Without worry
Or worried, searching in silence
For the way out.
And the vomit that I collected
For two thousand years,
From them
And from my own hunger,
Submerges every question.
The question of

To be or not to be
Is not the limit of the question,
But the future, open on the horizon,
Asking in its openness
About the way out.

56. CALL OF A NATION

Go!
Die on the field, my son.
What good is it that we live
And the world
Cannot build a house for me,
Cannot bring me a thing?
No road to the homeland,
No green land from my homeland.
Who knows
If there is any green left in my land
Or a flower,
Bashfully asking about me
And about a dawn in my son's eye.
For the bitter wind
Is still invading the world.
Who knows
If it had left anything
Of what my hand has planted,
Living in my homeland.

* * *

Die, my son,
Die in the field, my son.
Be my road to the homeland.
Perhaps, dead,
You will build me a house
Lasting for ages in my eye.
And you will live
Despite death with the green
In that flower,
In tomorrow's dawn.
Die, my son,
As long as you die to live.

57. DREAM OF THE SNOW

"She said, I have never felt a man's eye turning me into a piece of flesh
without turning stiff, and a cruel piece of wood, like death."

Reproach at a dismal hour—a fancy of the poet

Be, even for a moment,
Blood, mouth, hell,
Casting in your eyes
A thousand hidden desires.
Be a woman,
O disappointment,
Dying behind extinguished windows.
Be a woman
So the snow in your eyes
Could once dream of a heater.

58. AT THE CROSSROADS

"I know how worthless I have become in your eyes. . . .
Say it in whisper, and we shall not mention the matter again."

From a Yellow Letter

Do not worry,
We shall pass by . . . and not meet,
Our two roads will end at the crossroads.
All I have forgotten in my calm
Of pleasant dreams
And letters which aged without growing leaves.
Of visions
I restored to you . . . do not worry.
Do not panic at drying shreds,
Do not fear.
Perhaps if a winter
Should pass tomorrow
By your deserted door
In dismal, wretched silence,
You might find what you burn,
You might find what warms a sad silence,
You might find whatever remained
Of letters that aged but did not grow leaves,
A warmth for this closed world,
For your wearied heart.

* * *

— And you?
As for me — my oar is still in my boat.
The sea is still a dreamy expanse,
Calling,
And I might ask about the infinite.
— And you — ?
— You did not understand — ?
Close, then, my door,
And do not worry.

59. A CHILD OF THE FIRST WAR

In the year of brown bread,
In the year of avid nights,
Like yellow locust,
My mother gave birth
To my bloodied face.
And I grew up, with the first war, a wound,
And licked my blood.
I grew up, grew up, and my name
Became a number, not knowing my name.
And I knew the first war
In the brown bread
In the eyes of a dead one, not buried,
In a thousand arms,
Crucified in a notebook.
I grieved for my mother,
For my bloodied face
Wrapped in brown bread,
Cast as a promise to yellow locust.

* * *

O my mother,
My eyes grew larger,
My world became a larger talk,
Larger than a house my hands built on sand,
Larger — than
A child's joy,
With wings that flew with him, in a dream,
And larger than
My bloodied face.
For I, O my mother,
O shadow darkness of a murdered one not buried,
I ask about a meaning for my name
In my brown bread,
In the anger of avid nights like yellow locust.
And I, O mother,
Am searching in a bigger war

For a dead child
In the eye of a murdered one not buried.

* * *

In the year of brown bread,
My mother gave birth.
Generations of hunger
For brown bread
Gave birth in my bloodied face
To a bigger war.

60. NIGHT, COLD, AND WARDENS

At Al-Nugrah' prison,
The time was past ten,
The wardens will come.
A voice will shout:
Aḥmad, Salmān, 'Abbās . . .
And the silence dies.
—Hey, you—you—'Abbās:
Death is setting in Al-Nugrah' prison.
No mother is crying, no bells,
No branch wraps around a flower,
No name breathes in a rock,
No people.
For there, in the bitter land,
People die, and no people,
No wardens,
Night is long, O wardens,
The cold is cruel,
And the wound is deep,
O wardens.

* * *

Voices are humming in darkness.
—They died.
And sinks the darkness.
—Gone.
—Let them have rest.
—Is there no morning for this night?
We feel something like rancor.
A star is looming afar,
No cloud will pass by their world,
They are gone.
—A morning would peep.
In the morning the dead will not get up.
—Have they died?

The night is haunted by the wardens' sleep.
The night is long, O wardens,
The cold is cruel.
Revenge is bitter, O wardens.
Salmān did not die—nor Abbās.

* * *

On the ground,
The fetters' sound is serpents' hissing,
Twisting round a thousand arms,
Twisting round a thousand sails.
O my grudge,
O my rancor
Over the poisoned echo at Al-Nugrah.
No—
Do not wave farewell,
Stretch,
Stretch your hands,
As from a look,
From a tear burn,
From a branch that did not hug a flower,
From a name that was not carved on a rock,
We shall destroy your prison,
O Nugrah.

61. JOURNEY OF THE YELLOW LETTERS

For a thousand years,
O children of my dismal village,
We have been the yellow letters
In the Torah, the New Testament, and the Qur'ān.
We were the stiff dryness in the chisel,
Carving in your eyes our dubious shades.
The shades were
Worshiped in your depths,
Becoming history without men.
The letter will grow longer
Once it is a minaret,
Bending in supplication.
Once it is a church,
In the bleak mountains.
Once black gallows,
Or ropes,
Which your roads know,
In the dismal village.

* * *

For a thousand years,
We have been the yellow letters
In the New Testament,
The Old Testament, and the Qur'ān.
The letters were of soil,
Which every day materialized
Into blemished conception,
Into idols,
Into the lash and Sultan,
Into God and Devil,
But never once — into man.

* * *

For a thousand years,
O children of my dismal village,
We were in a trance with history,
Worshiping in your eyes
Our dubious shades.

* * *

And the journey comes to an end,
O my yellow letters,
Again we shall collect the lead,
Again we shall melt the lead
Into a prophetic tale,
Into a gun's hunger, a stupid song.
But we wouldn't find salvation
By a new yellow lie,
As our land is still a distance
Between our eyes, with no hope.

From *Songs of the Tired Guard*
(1971)

INTRODUCTION

I know how sad you are, O guard!
I know how tired you are, O guard!
And that the dawn you are expecting
Is still far away . . . but
Beware of falling asleep,
For the streets lit by thousands of lamps
Are still full of crime, falsehood, and deceit.
And you must watch everything
With a great deal of caution.
You may sing your sad songs,
All night long—but
Don't ever forget that you are responsible
For all this age,
Which may call on you
For salvation.

62. SLEEPING PILLS

Stop and read,
Do not cross.
Stop—beware!

* * *

What is in today's papers?
An advertisement in red.
Take a sleeping pill,
Take a pill,
A sleeping pill,
————I shan't read.
————I shan't beware.
I shall sleep without a sleeping pill.

* * *

The red light comes on.
A child is reading—hand me a pill.
A middle–aged man is reading . . . hand me a pi . . .
A girl is reading . . . a pill . . . a pill.
My mother wishes she could read.
O my mother,
We shan't read. . . . We shan't read . . . shan't . . .
We shall sleep without a sleeping pill.

* * *

Stop.
Halt . . .
What is in today's papers . . . ?
Nixon is addressing the council
About welfare and peace for the world.
What . . . !
A statement by Pope Paul
About welfare and peace for the world.

* * *

O darkness of Jerusalem!
Sleep in peace.
The world is talking of welfare and peace.
Bodies of killed children in Vietnam!
Sleep in peace.
The red line
Is like the red color,
Like the red light,
Asking about a sleeping pill.
Stop!
Halt . . .
What is in today's papers . . . ?
Nixon is addressing the council.
A statement by Pope Paul.
A bank is bankrupt.
Dancing in execution courts.
And the world in today's papers
Is talking about welfare and peace,
About a sleeping pill
For the killed in Vietnam,
For the killed in Jerusalem.
A child is reading . . . hand me a pill.
A middle-aged man is reading . . . hand me a p . . .
A girl is reading . . . pill . . . pill.
My mother wishes . . .
O my mother, sleep in peace,
The world is still
Talking about welfare and peace.

* * *

—Hand me a pill to sleep.
Take a pill, my son, to sleep.

* * *

The vendor's voice rattles.
It rolls.
The street quivers.
A wonderful thing,
Wonderful,
Sleeping pills.
Take a sleeping pill.

* * *

Hand me a pill—to sleep,
Hey, who, a pill to sleep.

* * *

And the street sleeps.
A wonderful thing—wonderful.
Sleeping pills.

63. INDICTED, THOUGH INNOCENT

In a room on the seventh floor,
They met . . .
Talked,
Wrestled,
Slept together,
And the curtain was dropped,
In a room on the seventh floor.

* * *

But I remained crucified by the wall,
And as you wanted me,
I remained like the nail,
Pushing in their eyes,
Pushing in their secret,
Pushing in the wall.
In a room on the seventh floor.

* * *

I heard her, sir,
Asking him of his wonderful love,
Of a body.
—Sorry, sir—
She said to him: It burns like fire.
It burns me like fire.
Once they talked about a lost world,
About a sperm in a lost world.
But I,
As you wanted me . . . as you created me,
Could not understand the dialogue,
Because I rose above their wonderful love,
Their body like fire.
And, as you warned me: "People are criminal."
"All are criminal."
"Even innocent love in the eyes."

And, as you wanted me,
I remained like a nail,
Pushing in their eyes,
Pushing in their secret,
Digging in the wall,
In a room on the seventh floor,
Searching in the whisper, the laugh, the dialogue,
For a time of revenge,
For the rebels' anger,
For a desire to be a rope round their necks,
And in their palms a nail.

* * *

Sorry, sir,
They were insistently innocent, innocent.

* * *

When the morning woke up in my town,
Penetrated the news bulletin,
A tale about a room on the seventh floor,
About a time for revenge,
About the rebels' rage.
And around their necks was a rope,
And in their palms a nail.

64. A CALL FOR STUPOR

Let the bells be silent,
And with your shoe-heel gouge out the sun
And extinguish people's eyes.
For in the town of dozing,
There is neither tomorrow nor yesterday.
And sleep,
You, the only one awake, like pain.
Hang on your rusty peg
What burdens you carry,
And sleep.
O you cast in repentance,
Peel off people's skins,
Leave them as their forest banquet;
For in the town of dozing
There is neither tomorrow nor yesterday.
You will not see in the blood drops
Abel, or your old prostitute,
Or the wedding virginity.
So sleep.
The big world behind the door
Has fallen asleep,
With no clock disturbing its sleep,
No figures.
And the dogs have fallen asleep,
So did the night,
The thieves and the guards.
So sleep,
Extinguish people's eyes,
And sleep.
Silence the bells.
Silence—the—
—ells,
S—S.

65. A DREAM IN FOUR SCENES

First Shot:
The screen is covered by two eyes.
Two lips open.
They smiled.
Several teeth glittered,
And the green color sinks in all colors.

* * *

Second Shot:
Two feet explore the night silently.
The knife glitters.
In the blade glitter visions,
For years and years.
Without sound
The two lips close,
With no sign of a kiss on the mouth.
Nothing but a drop of blood,
And the red color dives in all colors.

* * *

Third Shot:
Producer's name . . . You . . . Me . . . Them.
Director's name . . . You . . . Me . . . Them.
Viewer's name . . . You . . . Me . . . Them.
The screen is a dream space.
The killer, the killed, me.
Nothing but me.
A meaning,
Writing in a drop of blood.

* * *

Fourth Shot: From Outside,
The film dropped.
The producer escaped from a back door.

The viewer spat in my hand.
The film dropped.
Four shots drowned in a drop of blood.
But as I am the director,
The producer,
And the viewer,
I own nothing in the world
Except a dream space.
I have no house for my yearning,
No chest to hug,
No refuge anywhere.
And because
I have no refuge,
I know no coffee-shop,
No cabaret,
No brothel to accept me,
No woman in a tavern,
I shall stay here,
And wait for the second show.
The hall is empty except for one man, asleep.

66. EXPULSION

I was born behind the door.
I grew up
Behind the door.
And behind this door,
Many a time love in my body
Became paws and fangs.
How many a time, oh my blood shed to the earth,
O present in absence,
I was the killer,
And the killed!
I was the wound and the flies!
How many a time
I closed the door on me,
And slept, not dreaming,
Not asking,
Not looking for an answer,
Because I . . .
Do not worry,
The wolves will return,
The wolves will return
A second time,
A third time,
A fourth time.
Man will be born behind the door,
And we . . .
Do not worry. . . .
What remains is the small banquet,
The presence in absence.

67. THE KILLED WITNESS

Who killed the last resistance fighter?
I know who,
I know who gouged out his eyes,
Who severed his hands,
Who, your Highness,
Mutilated his large dream.
I know who,
For I have patronized that youth for years,
Before he was born in the vision and yearning,
Before he became a hideout in every corner,
Before he became all the love in his world,
All the earth in his vision.

* * *

Ah!
Before he became,
That young boy,
Wounds bleeding once,
And once
The wounds waiting in the knife.
I know who,
I know, your Highness
Who killed the last resistance fighter.

* * *

I know who,
For a thousand nights, I sat at his door,
I stayed up in the darkness of his eyelashes,
And became part of his bitter night.
And some of what lights in his exile.
And a thousand times
I was the muddy blood in his eyelashes.

* * *

I know who.
—Who killed the last resistance fighter?
Who killed the—
—I know who.
—Say who.
—Who is who.
—If I said who,
I would be, your Highness,
The witness killed as the last resistance fighter.

* * *

You and I, O Prince,
You, and I.

68. APOLOGY

Apology, our revered guests!
The announcer lied in his last bulletin.
For in Baghdad
There is no sea,
No pearls, no island.
All that Sindbad related
About the Genie Queens,
The emerald and coral islands,
About thousands from the Sultan's hands,
Is a myth woven by summer heat
In my little town.
From the shade burning at noon,
From the absence of stars,
In its nights silence,
When we had
The sea, shells, and white pearls,
The brilliant moon,
And the return of the fisherman in the evening.
In them we had,
In the announcer's lie in his last bulletin,
Our naïve dreaming paradise.
For we, our revered guests,
Lie, in order to be born anew,
Lie, to remain in our lengthy history,
Where we had
The sea, shells, white pearls,
And the hour of birth.

* * *

Apologies, our revered guests!
The announcer lied in his last bulletin.
For in Baghdad
There is no sea, no pearls, and no island.

69. BETWEEN TWO POINTS

The wind does not frighten us
If it howled,
Or howled in growling.
The night behind our closed door
Remains a moonlit land,
So long as I have across my past scattered roads,
A space, asking me about a rendezvous,
A rendezvous that stretches to a thousand tomorrows,
So long as I have,
In every vein of my stiffened hand,
A tale unborn,
And in its everlasting darkness
I still dream to become
Some sandalwood,
Burned in a censer.

70. DIALOGUE IN THE BEND

Have you not slept, O sad guard!
When will you sleep,
You who stays up in our lamp
These thousand years?
O you, who are crucified
Between his two open palms, for years,
Don't you sleep?
—For the twentieth time, I want to sleep.
I fall in sleep but cannot sleep.
For the fiftieth time,
I fell in sleep but could not sleep.
For sleep with the sad guard
Remains like the knife edge.
I am afraid to sleep,
I am afraid I may wake up in dreams.
Let them burn Rome, let them burn Berlin,
Let them steal the China wall,
You do have to sleep!
It is time for this sad guard
To lean for a minute and sleep.
I sleep!
And in every moment,
Berlin is still burning, and every hour,
A wall from China is stolen.
Between a moment and another,
A dragon is born.
I am afraid to sleep,
For sleep with the sad guard
Remains like the knife edge.

71. CONFESSIONS FROM 1961

I shan't go.
I won't go.
How wretched it is to spend all my life
In a dark office:
The same face cast on the black desk,
The same flabby time in the shade,
The same smooth papers,
The same letter asking about a letter,
And on the wall, there is still
The name of God,
Trying to open its eyes, stretch its arms.
It says:
Come to me you who are dying,
In the name of man.
The two Cufic letters hang down.
God dangles by two letters from the ceiling.
Who is crucified by His two letters?
Who is crucified?
Answer me, oh arms avarice.
My face cast on the black table
Has wearied me,
And I am tired of signing on lies,
Which will be broadcast
Morning and evening.
And I hated my empty mottos.

* * *

How wretched it is to go,
How wretched it is to spend all my life
In a dark office,
Crucified between the two Cufic letters,
Between a letter asking about a letter.

* * *

As yesterday, I went.
My janitor opens the room doors,
Bends his thirsty figure,
With the anxiety of someone
Trained by hunger to bend his figure,
And lowers his greeting to a whisper.
He will say: Good morning.
Good morning . . . is a name of a singer,
No, name of the poem,
No, name of a newspaper,
I know it,
I know its owner . . . he was my friend.
One day he gifted me Al-Mutanabbi's *Diwān*,
The Barqooqi edition.
He spoke to me about a dawn
That may come lightning like a sword,
Mortal like a sword.
He spoke to me about a meaning
Further than the shape of the letter.

* * *

I answer: Good morning
The coffee . . . I take it on the balcony.
Close the room door.
The coffee . . . do not forget . . . bitter.
And I hate it bitter.
I hate this black tar.
I hate this black road at the bottom of the cup.
And I hate even the black ink . . .
Even the two Cufic let . . .
—Do not blaspheme,
your Lord will not pardon this idea.
—Bitter.

—Yes . . . bitter.
One with diabetes does not like his coffee
Except bitter.
—How did you get it and when?
—Do not ask.
I remembered our residential quarter,
The school,
Our teacher of religion:
No Q and A in religion.
Did you understand, pupils?
But we did not then . . . did not understand.
And we grew up.
We became bigger than fearing the curved C.
Bigger than being wounded by the sword,
And we saw all children's fingers in our quarters
Pointing to us:
Bless you, revolution's faces,
Bless you, twentieth-century faces.
—How did you get it and when?
Oh, if you knew.
That revolution in the twentieth century
Gives the rebels nothing but diabetes,
An ulcer,
And bitter coffee.
And I was among the rebels
And knew sleeping on cold cement floors,
Like the twentieth century.
I knew the rebel jailers,
I knew the rebel jailed,
And I knew that the revolution
Might pluck out my nails,
Might crucify a Ḥallāj [Al-Ḥallāj] in my chest every morning.
I felt their fingers in my eyes saying:
You are cursed, and be food for fire,
For diabetes, ulcer, bitter coffee,
And revolution.

They became these two Cufic letters
And this head cast on the desk for years.

* * *

My janitor did not understand a thing.
He greeted, and left,
Greeting the revolution in the two letters.
He greeted the revolution in my cast head,
Then bent his thirsty figure,
And anxiously
He closed the door on me . . .
On the two Cufic letters,
On the name of Go . . .
And we sank in the room's silence.

* * *

But behind the closed doors,
The janitor's son was preparing for the revolution.
The janitor's son was himself the revolution.
Who knows,
He may not drink his coffee . . . bitter.

Al-Ḥallāj, A mystic of the Abbasid period (585–922)

72. HEY . . . YOU ARE INDICTED

I went out tonight,
And in my pocket, I had ten I.D.s
That allow me to go out tonight.
My name: Buland, son of Akram,
And I come from a well-known family.
I never killed anybody,
Never robbed anybody,
And in my pocket, I have ten I.D.s as my witnesses.
So why can't I go out tonight?

* * *

The sea was without shores,
Darkness was larger than man's eyes,
Deeper than man's eyes.
The street pavement was empty
Except for the clicks of my shoes:
Click . . . click . . . click.
I gathered my shadow in a lamp once,
And once I scattered it.
Then I laughed because
I realized that
I own my shadow,
And I can cast it behind me,
Can dump it in a pool of muddy water,
Can crush it under my shoes,
Can suffocate it between my clothes.
Click . . . click . . . click.
And the shadow behind me,
Click . . . click.
The shadow behind me . . . behind me . . . behind me.
How great is your shadow of a man
Who has ten I.D.s
In a Time that has no I.D.?

* * *

I sang, whistled, shouted,
Laughed, laughed, laughed.
And I felt that I own all the sea, all the night,
All the black pavements,
And that I can now force them to listen to me,
To be an echo of my call,
To be part of my shoe-click sound.
Click . . . click . . . click.
I stuck in my hand,
My ten I.D.s are still in my pocket.
Here is my name.
Here is my picture.
Here is the stamp of the police chief in my country.
Here is the signature of the justice minister,
Proudly stretched to cut through my mouth,
And fell one of my teeth,
Scratch part of my address.
And I feared to . . . and swallowed my tongue,
For I have seven more I.D.s,
I swear, if a mountain passed by them,
It would bow its height and say:
They are the great: About my poetry,
My letters, knowledge, art,
And because I carry ten I.D.s in my pocket,
I sang, whistled, shouted,
Laughed . . . laughed . . . laughed.
How great is your shadow of a man
Who carries ten I.D.s in a Time that has no I.D.

* * *

On the following day,
There were two policemen at my door.
They asked me: Who are you?
Me?

Buland, son of Akram,
And I am from a well-known family.
I never killed anybody,
Never robbed anybody.
I have, in my pocket, ten I.D.s
For my witness,
And that . . . so why . . . ?

* * *

They laughed at me . . . at all my ten I.D.s,
And I saw a hand flashing in my eye,
Falling between disappointment and cowardice.
—Hey, you are indicted!
—Hey, you!
What have they done to my name,
My picture, the signature of the justice minister?
I did not know . . .
But
I realized that my I.D.s were nothing but false witnesses,
And that I will sleep tonight
In prison, in the name of my I.D.s.
And I laughed . . . laughed . . . laughed.

* * *

In a Time that has no I.D.,
He will be indicted who owns any I.D.
Tear them . . . tear them, my jailer,
Crash them, crash them, my jailer.
And I heard his steps behind me:
The sea was his . . . the night was his,
With all the black pavements,
Click . . . click . . . click.

73. DIALOGUE IN THREE DIMENSIONS

O all of you,
O absence of these present,
You will pass every moment by my darkened house,
Bearing the burden of my heavy night
In your hypocritical silence!
Here I am, dying for years,
Creeping for years,
A thread of blood between the wound and the knife.
—Sleep, you madman—we want to sleep!
—Sleep you damned—we want to sleep!
We want to be liberated by the dark!

* * *

O, you justice, hanging around the necks of the dead,
O, you,
Black shroud in ancient vaults,
Shout at them:
They lied!
For there is nothing between falsehood and truth
Except blood that dried on the asphalt years ago;
Dried, so it won't be remembered
By the wound nor recognized by the knife.
Shout at them:
"Tomorrow when the morning passes by us,
The knife and the wound will meet,
With the spot of blood carried by the passers' shoes.
Another sin without sinners."
Shout at them:
"Tomorrow when the jailed cell wakes up,
If the jailed and jailer meet,
Two faces will show in their eyes:
God, and Satan,
And nothing but the callous walls

Is the pale witness.
Nothing but an aperture that had teeth.
—Sleep, madman!
—Sleep, Be damned!
The echo is tired, the space is closed
To your sad cries.
The jailer woke up in the jailed.
—Sleep, madman, sleep.
We want to sleep.
We want to be liberated by the dark.
Joint Chorus
O Lord! O Lord! O Lord!
Thou knowest that we are neither of these nor of those
And that we are thy face in hope,
Thy decree in eternity.
So do not blame the witness for what he saw
Nor the hearer for what he heard.
It is by the ear thou gavest us we heard,
And by the eye thou grantest us we saw,
And the eye cannot have enough of seeing,
And the ear cannot have enough of hearing.
By thy will, based on justice,
We shall speak the truth.
Women's Chorus
Hallelujah! Hallelujah!
In thy name he was born,
In thy name he was martyred, in times of hardship,
When he knew thee in absolute freedom,
When he knew himself in the fettered slave,
He turned to thee
And turned away from thee.
When he then, through thee, rebelled against thee,
He was killed, was martyred.
O Lord! O Lord! O Lord!
In thee he exceeded thy heaven,

In himself diminished thy hell.
So he is neither of thy heaven
Nor of thy hell.
So accept him as a martyr for thy cause.
Joint Chorus
Thy forgiveness, O Lord!
In this voice we are none but thee,
Nor in that voice but thee.
We are none but thy right in this voice,
And in that.
We come together in desire
And die in hope.
If we hear, thou art the hearer,
If we see, thou art the one who sees.
Men's Chorus
Hallelujah! Hallelujah!
They knew thee in the distance.
So thou wert the Lord and they the slaves.
He who wanted thy freedom
Stripped it from thee and killed thee.
Let him be killed for what he desired.
O Lord! Freedom is a need.
He who realizes himself in the slave, within him,
Transcended to himself in the freeman within thee.
So that the cleavage may be
All the promise of reunion
Between Lord and slave.
Women's Chorus
In the name of the Lord, he was born,
In His name he was martyred.
So, there was the man.
Men's Chorus
In the name of the Lord, they dealt justice,
In His name they killed.
So there was the man.

Joint Chorus

O Lord! O Lord! O Lord!
We are neither of these nor of those.
We are neither of thy martyrs,
No more of thy warriors.
We are none but the letter that listens,
None but the letter that sees.
We are none but thy span,
In the step of thy man across the earth;
Thy span in the wakefulness that every evening sleeps.
Thy span in the questioning throes in a thousand hopes.
Hallelujah! Hallelujah! Hallelujah!

* * *

The hall is the same hall,
With its seats,
Its summoner's voice,
With its hunting hounds' eyes,
Pierced in their victims' flesh.
The same white collars,
The same glossy shoes,
And the time curdled in the clock,
Still as—
—Quiet—do not speak!
There is the sign,
Still the same sign,
From the Ottoman era:
"Justice is the basis of governance."
What—?
"Justice is the basis of governance."
—Quiet—Do not speak.
Lies—lies—lies—lies!
Governance is the basis of justice.
To own a knife gives you the right to kill me.
—Quiet—Do not speak!

What liars — What condemned!
"Justice is the basis of governance."
I can almost laugh, except that I am
Settling in doubt
And can almost cry.
— Quiet — Do not speak — Do not speak — Do not —
— Quiet — Quiet!

* * *

And I kept quiet.
Here I am falling in my first dimension,
My case is sinking in my face,
My eye is searching for my eye.
Here I am, torn between two:
A silent man in a questioning child.

* * *

In the name of the Lord,
In the name of the People,
In the name of the Law,
We shall try this face, grim as a wasteland,
Desolate as a curse.
We shall nail his palms on the door of the hall.
We shall dig paradise in his eyes.
— How great is thy justice, my Lord!
How great is the injustice of the killer
In thy name, oh my People!
How wide my sway!
For my sake was resurrected the buried promise,
For my sake
They became the Lord, the People, and the Law.
And for my sake,
All shall be without guilt.
For I alone am the killed for killing my father.
Like me is the guilt, alone.

* * *

—What is your name?
—I know no name—I don't remember my name.
My mother died, and I was not yet born,
With a meaning in my name.
And since I had no name,
I knew not what my mother was . . . illed my father.
—Did you kill your father?!
—Killed your father—kill—?
'lled my father.
Name the killer Maḥmood or Aḥmad,
Mas'ood or As'ad,
Give him a name to bring him nearer to crucifixion,
For the criminal's blood is a feast to the Lord.
—What did you say? What do you pronounce?
—Death—Death—Death—Death.
Death should be in the name of the Lord.
Death should be in the name of the People.
Death should be in the name of the Law.
—Wash not your hands, for you shall not regret.
For crime is cleansed by blood.
Blood—Blood—Blood—Blood.
—There is the Hall, the same old Hall,
From the Ottoman era.
"Justice is the basis of governance."
I can almost laugh, except that
I am settling in doubt,
I can almost—
Cry.
Women's Chorus
O Lord! O Lord! O Lord!
Here we are, like thee, in repetition born,
In habit we live on.
Like thee in the departing summer
And the approaching summer.

Like thee in the stone falling in death,
Without tragedy.
Like thee in the furrows of the plough.
O Lord!
Thou didst set us apart,
So we saw the whole,
But lost thy secret in the parts.
We became thy right in the killer
Since we became thy right in the killed,
For the furrow lines are alike:
They wound as they go,
And they wound as they return.
The two wounds are but one hope.

Women's Chorus
Hallelujah — Hallelujah!
The moment he was born in desire,
He forgot thee in the threat of fire,
Of tar and terror.
So her breasts dried up,
And his lips dried on her breasts,
As he questioned them about her,
As he sought the face of his father
To find the killer of his mother.
They screamed in his face:
What is your name? Your name?
Whoever has no name has no mother.
Whoever has no name is disavowed by his fatherhood.
— Give me a name to become your love on earth,
To become with it a promise of love.
They said to him, "Our names are our crosses,
Our torments,
Our dreams.
By them the Lord shall know us on the day of judgment.
We will not grant them, unless we know
Your face in the killer or in the killed."

O Lord! Their rancor has cast him into exile.
He was denied their ground.
They pulled out their land from under his steps,
So he became thee,
The killer and the killed.
Joint Chorus
O Lord! O Lord! O Lord!
Thou who hast heard with our ear,
Thou who hast seen with our eye,
Bless them in murder,
For had it not been in thy name,
They would not have killed.
Thou broughtst them nearer to thee,
Becoming, as thy light fell on them,
Their vow for justice — justice were they.
The one who denied Thee was among them.
And he was rightly convicted.
Thou didst narrow their distance.
The part was the whole with them.
The criminal is he who does not know Thee,
In this part or that part.
How is it, then, with someone who did not climb a mountain
To bless the meekness of the soul,
To bless those who inherit the earth,
To say to them:
"Blessed be ye in hunger,
In thirst,
In grief,
In the rain falling in the name of the Lord."
To say to them:
"The salt of the earth shall not decay."
O Lord! O Lord! O Lord!
If thou acceptst him as a martyr,
To thy just cause
Accept them in murder,
As a way to truth!
Hallelujah — Hallelujah — Hallelujah!

* * *

What are you dreaming of, O paths of ashes?
What visions have made your eyes
The land of God, the promised land?
So they extended as two verdant roads?
And you were
All the earth, all the gracious heaven,
In these two roads.
Blessed be you!
How spacious the sky between two winks of the eyes!
How cheap the heaven, when bought on credit!
Then fall asleep,
For the chatter of woods does not ask for ears.
So fall asleep.
In the path of ashes, night becomes
The land of God and the promised land.
In two eyes it becomes
Two verdant roads.
And shout,
Shout as you wish in my face,
Cast under the locust feet,
At my hand, nailed
To the body joining its fire,
To the dreamer behind the censer.
As you will, shout:
You lied. . . . They did not lie,
They did not crucify the truth
Though they have crucified our Christ.
For our road is not a black alley
Nor blood on a black alley.
Tell us, ye paths:
"You lied — they did not,
For truth is not a street that goes around a town
Like a rope,
Nor is it an avaricious hand.
Right is that bright passage
Across falsehood, dreams, and silence."

Tell us, you, fraud:
"Sleep, as we sleep, to reach
The land of God, the promised land."
Tell us:
"Truth is not a line dividing death from birth.
Sleep as we sleep
So the two roads may bring back
The truth you seek, as white as dreams.
Your eyes are still laden
With the drowsiness they bear,
With rapturous minarets and bells.
With a road to God, without jails or wardens.
Sleep as we sleep.
How spacious the sky between two winks of the eye!
How cheap the heaven when bought on credit!

* * *

You lied — lied — lied.
— Sleep, you Be damned!
You made us tired, you wearied, killed us.
Sleep, you Be damned, we want to sleep!
We want to be liberated by the dark!
Do not wake the jailer in the jailed.
— I swear never to sleep.
My eyes may perish, but I shall never sleep.
I sneer at two verdant roads,
In the paths of ashes.
I am the blood that dried on the asphalt
Years ago.
The wound knows it,
The knife will not deny it.
I am the death that comes like birth.
Women's Chorus
O God!
Thou hast made my resurrection
My words of consolation in times of hardship

And a call of love on the day of wrath.
How unjust thy individual man
When he made thee in his image,
To barter thy glory, that eternal glory,
For the vanishing face of man.
They were against thee
The moment they thought they had thy love
And pleased thy affection.
In thy name they said:
"Let this disobedient son perish,
This one who desires to be thy equal
In eternal glory."
In him they perished,
In them he was eternalized.
Man lived a yearning in man,
They died in the paleness of his hands
And the silence of his eyes.
That was thy will,
Thy wish in the way that has become two roads:
The one hides itself from itself
And returns to its past.
The other reveals itself in itself,
And the two roads are
Thy promise to preserve
And thy threat to annihilate.
The first falls outside for the bodies to become temples.
If they grow old,
They will grow old in the shade thy prophecy,
Becoming a stone,
Hiding behind its thickness
The earthworms,
Banquets of worms,
The other, thyself without a temple.
O Lord, who art in man,
Spare him the rancor lurking in fires,
Spare him thy threat in hatred

And in dread, in curse.
He who declines thy pledge of heaven
Retains thee on earth as love.
Hallelujah—Hallelujah.
Women's Chorus
Lord, hear us!
No excuse has this man.
His ears were blocked,
So he heard not thy bells, O Lord!
His eyes were blinded,
So he saw thee not behind the crosses,
Aye, Lord!
His lips denied thy gifts, so
Therefore, he was the loser in that denial.
He was—he was—he was—
No excuse has this man,
We have seen him
And saw his dagger deep in his father's heart.
We heard that the victim's blood was
Hooting like an owl,
Asking about thee and in thee.
O Lord!
Patricide is larger
Than all their seven sins.
O Lord!
Have no mercy on him, lest mercy
Become a haven for the murderer,
The thief, and the fugitive.
A haven for the thief who rubs,
From his father's house,
The legacy of man to man.
O Lord, who art eternal in the word of justice,
Who art hard,
Like fetters; obstinate like murder!
Our God, who art eternal in the word that says:

"Be
Like the departing summer
And the approaching summer,
Like the stone falling in death,
Without tragedy.
What remains of thy earth
If the sons, against their fathers, rebel?
What remains of thy earth
If the present that past negates?
When purity resembles filth?
With what wouldst thou feed thy fire,
On judgment day?
Why do dreamers dream of heaven,
O Lord!
If thou wouldst forgive,
Why didst thou create sin?
Hallelujah — Hallelujah — Hallelujah.

* * *

Because I had no name,
Knew no mother,
I turned the milk of the shriveled breast into poison.
I died from it one day,
I lived on it one day,
Growing into a question: "What is my name?"
Who was my father?
Who was my mother?
O people, grant me a name,
A name to bear me as a threat,
A cloud,
Rain foreboding death.
Give me a name:
Mas'ood or As'ad, Maḥmood or Aḥmad
A name to draw me near to God,
A name to draw me near to the cross.

A name — a name — a name.
For, people, I am without a name,
I am a dagger deep in my father's heart.

* * *

I knocked at the doors, one by one.
I bribed the doorman,
I begged a woman,
A child, an old man, a young man,
They answered not.
No door was opened, no window was closed.
If evening came,
I became a pavement on this road,
Trampled by their feet,
Turned white once, turned black another time.
If morning came,
I became a worthless garbage heap,
A rotten loaf of bread
In the hands of a hungry child.
I wept here,
I wept there,
I loafed here,
I loafed there,
Searching for myself at a lost address.
Thousands of names passed by:
Paintings, colors, lights,
Names choked by white collars,
Names sweating under black coats,
House names,
Countless street names
Passed by . . . no one asked me:
"Who made you cry?
Where did you come from?
Which milk wetted your mouth?"
. . . No one!
A garbage heap is worthless.
The street pavement is no one.

* * *

Here I am,
Falling in my second dimension,
My eye searching in my father's eye
For the death of a man.
Here I am,
Torn between two:
This one cast by the road,
Implored by a woman for help:
"Kill him — kill him — kill him,"
And that one deep in penitence, down to sin.

* * *

O, my mother's face,
Banished without a crust of bread
Or a drop of water.
Why did you come back?
Have you not realized
That you have died, like everything else,
And rusted, like everything else?
Why, then, did you come back to me?!
Nothing I have but my cowardice,
And my cries bound to my ears.
Why did you come back, why back, why . . . ?
O, my mother's banished face,
Tear off your face from mine,
Pull off your hand from mine,
Suffice it to be
The fall in your eye, another banished face
In the bare desert,
Poorer than bare desert,
Poorer than a crust of bread
Or a drop of water.
So why did you come back to me?
Nothing I have!

74. PROCESSION OF THE SEVEN SINS

(1)

Once I ran after my shadow,
Trying to catch it,
Trying to be in it completely.
When I bent,
It bent like me,
Staring like me
At an old fragment of my infant face,
Which has remained without place or time,
Remained without shadow.

(2)

I dream
To refuse to be born in a thermal scale
Because
I know that night and day
Will not ask whether I am
In ice
Or in fire.

(3)

Yesterday,
When I was born in a dubious woman's bag,
I realized in her mirror
What I did not know of her terrible secrets.
I realized
That her earth is smaller than a bag.

(4)

When we wake or sleep,
We dig, not in the earth
Nor search in ruins
For our faces buried among a heap of bones,
Nor will our age be measured
By a skull, where years dried up in its ugliness.
We are here a distance
That cannot, in figures, reckon how to grow or wane,

As on its way lies no town,
Born in the morning's cry for help,
Or die with the fall of dark.
And in our years,
There are no days.

(5)

When the seas submerge our dream serenity,
With the current we glide
Like sails,
Carrying, in their yearning,
Pearls, coral, and shells,
Or a small child's wish,
To frolic on virgin shores,
Untouched by a storm.

(6)

I am a woman,
Born in a lengthy, wintry night.
So I shut my room door,
Lock my window to the winds, stars, and echo.
So my house became a hearth,
And I slept to be born, every moment, in a death.

(7)

In order to remain dreaming,
Should your Messiah come to us,
We would be, as he wanted us:
Murmuring prayers.
Should you allow his crucifixion,
We will be his nail and merciless fire.
Suffice for us, of all he had,
All he wished for us,
Vacant masks that neither weep nor smile.

75. CALL OF THE SEVEN SINS

You repeated,
A thousand times,
That we are false,
False are our days,
False is our god,
And that our door's keyhole
Has no key,
And that
It was neither by sun conceived,
Nor by winds violated,
And that it was nothing
But the way of death and oblivion.
A thousand, thousand times
You told us that there would never be for us
A promise in the morning,
That we are . . . false,
That we are . . . lost,
That we have neither earth nor sun,
That we are dreamers.
Do you not know that we are
The sun that warms us,
The earth that bears us,
The morning that we wish to be,
So, turn off your lamps, you madman!
We want to sleep,
We want to be liberated by the dark.
Joint Chorus
O Lord! O Lord! O Lord!
Wouldst thou forgive us our trespasses!
For we are here like these or those,
Settling in both their voices,
Getting lost in the narrow distance
Between their eyes.

We wanted to see . . . but did not see.
We wanted to hear . . . but did not hear,
For the earth is distances, O Lord!
The earth is distances,
And each distance
Has dimensions that may start from this eye,
But not from that eye,
May set out from this touch,
But not from that touch.
Truth is dimension moving things:
Between man and the shadow of man,
Between time embedded inside
And time clotted outside.
O Lord! Whoever kept far from thee
Has not seen thee.
O Lord! Whoever came closer to thee
Has not seen thee.
Whoever proclaims: "I am the Lord"
Has not seen thee.
O Lord! O Lord! O Lord!
Wouldst thou forgive us our trespasses!
For thou,
Thou didst set men as boundaries,
The one negating the other,
To make death thy eternity on earth.
O Lord!
In love and in hate,
Accept us as just witnesses,
Who saw nothing, heard nothing,
Realized nothing except your dimension among things,
Becoming hope in some heart,
Death in another.
The one eternal like death is thou,
O Lord!
Hallelujah—Hallelujah!

* * *

If I feared,
With my hunger I sheltered my fear
And outgrew my weakness.
If I hungered,
I fed on my hunger
And stretched my arm to the hungry behind me
And outgrew my weakness.
If my lip dried, parched like a summer noon,
I would cut a wound in my palm
To hide my voice therein,
To hide my lips therein,
And would look,
Awaiting it to be wet in the time of bleeding.
And my weakness I outgrew.

* * *

I walked the ways of men,
Picking up their steps,
Picking up their dreams,
Whatever they drop, figure or letter,
So I learned
That the thieves are the other face of the guards,
That, among people,
I am the two faces of this slave
And that slave-trader.
Also, I learned that, in the lofty mountain,
I am an edge.
So I outgrew my weakness,
Was not humbled,
Was not shamed,
And was not but
The death waiting at the edge of the sword,
The hatred lurking in hunger and fear.
So, time of bleeding, liberate me.
Bring down your devil from my shoulder.

I'll demolish their mountains,
Destroy their caves,
Raise my death in theirs.
—Quiet, don't speak.
—Don't speak.
—Hush . . . don't.
I shall not stop speaking, shall not, not.
O you, the stone falling in death with no tragedy,
Be my death,
To be born in the time to come,
Be a wound in my palm,
Be a serpent in my voice,
Be thou the God, man without death.

* * *

What did you say, what do you pronounce?
Death — death — death — death.
Death in the name of the People,
Death in the name of the Law

* * *

I hate to be hanged at the crossroad.
—You shall be hanged, stoned, burned at the crossroad.
You shall not be a sign to a village
Nor the quest of a town
Nor the wish where our roads meet.
You shall not be a hand
Seeking for its blood warmth in my hand.
Here at the crossroad,
Tomorrow you should be
A passage for the wind, the sound, and dusk.
You shall end.
No forehead were you,
No blood, no mouth,
Nothing but ashes of the dreams you were
And of that cast off . . .

—Yea, that cast-off who crumbled,
Lighted a way, then expired.
—You lied—No,
Nothing but a corpse for the hungry hawk,
Nothing but a skull through which
Whistles the wind,
Nothing but a funeral,
A dead man cast at the crossroad.

* * *

O people!
O rapturous minarets, O bells,
Who would build a fire for him?
—I, I, I, I . . .
Who would gather stones to stone him?
—I, I, I, I . . .

* * *

O people!
O my other face in man,
O my other face in nail and fire,
When . . . O when
Shall you realize that he who came
Shall, by your living passion, remain alive,
Sending, from your piercing nail, a prophet?
—You lie, you lunatic,
You lie, for the nail is the hammer's way.
—You blaspheme, you damned.
O my other face in man,
Until when
Shall you, but once, for me become
A stalk of corn,
And once, for me become
Death and a gallows rope?
Joint Chorus
O Lord! O Lord! O Lord!
We saw something we could not grasp.

We saw a truth we could not comprehend.
A woman's face carved on the mountain
Near the crossroad.
In her eyes we saw two water fountains,
A moon, stars, and a sky.
And we saw the naked body,
Despite the hungry hawk,
The cursed wind, the darkening night,
Despite the nail and despite the fire,
Changing to a verdant land.
We heard a voice,
Not coming from thy earth, O Lord!
Not coming from that ominous fire, O Lord!
Not from thy destined heaven, O Lord!
A woman's voice saying:
My son was not hanged,
My son did not die.
Who died, then, near the crossroad, O Lord?
Who died, then, near the crossroad?
And the woman,
That woman, who was she, O Lord?

76. STOLEN FRONTIERS

O my homeland!
How could you let a filthy slave-driver
Pull me by the ear
And tour with me in every town,
A slave offered for sale
At the lowest price at hand?
Is it because, oh my greater homeland,
I have imagined you great
And vowed
I should not recognize a homeland for myself
That does not grow
Except as a bashful map
In a notebook
And black letters that know nothing but
Braying on this platform
Or hooting on that platform?

* * *

Is it because,
O my poor homeland,
I have imagined you great
And vowed
I should not recognize a homeland for myself,
Divided between the knife
And cattle that do not open their eyes
Except to the glitter of the knife?
O my homeland,
O memory of rotten sand,
O face of my son exiled, with no homeland.
O disappointment of a history
That had no promise in time,
O falsehood of a fig leaf,
Is it because
I have imagined you

And vowed
I should not recognize a homeland for myself,
As a shroud,
As gallows and deserts,
Growing nothing but skulls of the hanged,
I vowed to recognize a homeland for myself,
Not a prison, not a child's whoop
Or a fetter's force
Or a dragon's eyes.

* * *

Is it because,
O my homeland,
I have imagined you great,
You have closed my house windows
In my face
And stolen your frontiers,
All your frontiers from me,
So I can be like you, my homeland,
A slave offered for sale
At the lowest price at hand?
How miserable I am
In the exiled promise of no time!
What miserable time I am,
Smaller than a hungry child's palms
Smaller than a dream in a lost man's eyes.
Smaller than thirst, seeking to cool off in the shade!

77. SINDBAD'S EIGHTH JOURNEY

O you, sailor,
O you, inquiring about a shadow of yours,
Forgotten for a month by land.
You cannot close your eyes,
Ashamed to face your death,
Cast on the roadside.
All roads in the land are equal for the dead.
So open your eyes — and die.
In your death be greater than atonement,
Greater than being born dead in a dog's paradise
Of promised brides of gold
And paradises of lies . . .
To the last drop of light in his eyes
He stretches out his hands,
Saying: Wait.
O star of a dawn wet by tears. . . . Wait,
Here I am coming
From the remotest memory in my mirror,
About a man who sailed all over the world,
All over the world's skies,
All over the world's skies and the world's seas,
All over love and hatred.
But they were nothing more than a sea smaller than a drop,
Too small to make up the desert. (1993)

78. ON THE VERGE OF THE FALLEN WORLD

I feel dizzy,
I feel that the earth which I loved,
Even here,
Is lustfully biting my cat's eye,
And a craving in my neighbor's dog's eye.
Falling,
Sinking in a bottomless well,
Shouting to me:
Don't come near the fence,
Our land is collapsing,
The sun will fall, so don't,
Don't come near the fence,
Don't shut the lock.
Hold onto the remains of the breath
In its attempts to escape.
Can the sun fall?
The sun I knew as a long tale
Of the sands, stars, and sea journeys,
The journey of the morning across our house,
Her house
And a thousand, thousand houses?
Can the sun fall?
The sun I knew, in the diver's look, for years,
In the shell's call for help?
I bring my feet together
In a sarcastic howl,
I should pull down the sky,
Extinguish the stars,
Kick off the clouds.
I shall kill death — yes,
Kill that tyrannical adulterer.
I shall kill it,
Plant my teeth in its blue carcass.
I shall burn it, drag it

From one street to another,
Make from its ashes
All my children's toys.
If you want me to love them . . . I shall love them.
If you want me to hang them . . . I shall hang them.
Make them dance,
Tattoo them on my arm
As a tale about a day of revenge.
I'll kick it . . . kill it,
Make of its blind eyes
Crescents and stars,
Dark paths . . . traps.
So the maze will expand.
It is time for us
To replace the mice by men in the maze.
I bring my feet together in a sarcastic howl,
A guffaw, a sunk bloodied mouth.
Can the sun fall . . . And it has not
Shouted at me through a thousand mouths:
Pain will turn a shark's bone in its throat.
Don't come near the fence.
Don't shut the lock.
Hold onto the remains of the breath
In its attempt to escape.

* * *

The sun will fall, and the day is not over,
Dark, black, like bitumen.

* * *

Dizziness . . . dizziness.
Suck me the thickness of walls,
Faces, distances and journeys turn down,
And the wall dims.

* * *

Dizziness . . . dizziness.
My hands travel in darkness and dust,
The sun turns as if it were
Dying in the grip of a spiderweb.
The wing is tossed by silence,
The silence explodes,
There . . . it is dying.
Here I am another fly dying.
I fall in the bottomless well,
No sun, no land, no day.
Another fly dies,
And the mercury settles in the thermometer. (October 28, 1995)

79. TWO VOICES LATE AT NIGHT

(1)

The street is still stretching its figure before me,
Black, taking me from one shade to another,
From one lamp
To another lamp, between them I sink
In a spot of dark mud.
I dive deep down in mud.
But I am still singing, playing with my shadow,
Without fear or hesitation.
Here I am
Enlarging my night and saying to my images:
Enlarge as disheveled forests,
Joining the dawn
With the patience sunk in my wounds' silence,
Far away from me,
From my home, my homeland,
Captive in the hand of a cutthroat,
Far from me,
And near me, as I am still singing,
Still here shining in my lamp's alienation,
In my shadow sinking more and more
In mud.

(2)

As in every evening,
I opened my window to the night stars.
They come to me without cover,
Barefooted except for a charged yellow glare,
Something smaller than some hope,
Some hope that my future
Will sleep on my hand,
As clear skies
And white suns and promises.

* * *

As on every morning,
I close my window against night and its horror,
Against black clouds.
I close my window, blind it, shut it,
I turn off all lights.
Nothing but me—nothing but the blind window.

* * *

How beautiful is night, filled with stars and suns,
With illusion, bringing you some hope.
How ugly is a morning
Drowning your eyes
With nothing behind them
Except your face involved in darkness,
Involved in your face, your silence, your death.
In that you won't know yourself
Except in a dream
That passed through a deep memory. (December 23, 1995)

80. I WILL STAY HERE

Let us depart together
To another country,
To a country that may have your color,
That black one,
Like the sun stuck in my color.
My lady, let us depart,
My lady, I'm tired
Of this insomnia, drowned in the darkness
Of the infested homeland.
It wearied me
That I nailed its darkness along my arm
And along my loss in the wild,
Along the cries of my people in that homeland.
It wearied me
That I vowed to my eye
That I will not cry for a lost homeland
Or a road that went astray
Or a home attacked by cactus,
So it became not my home.

* * *

Would you come with me, my lady,
O my pain deep in the silence of nights,
In the darkness of sins.

* * *

Who knows,
We may be born, my lady,
In another land,
Another homeland,
Children and boats of white dreams,
And nights within a thousand days.

* * *

A widowed woman said:
What about us?
You who are fleeing from us,
From all the murdered,
From all our graveyards, curbed behind the walls!

* * *

O my pain . . . won't you come with me?
—No, no.
I will stay here . . . who knows,
My homeland may ask me about my promise
Of revenge,
About my vow to avenge . . . who knows? (August 8, 1996)

BULAND AL-ḤAIDARI

(1926–1996) was a widely published Iraqi poet and literary critic.

'Abdulwāḥid Lu'lu'a

is professor emeritus of English literature at Philadelphia University
in Amman, Jordan, and the author and translator of seventy-one books,
including *Listen to the Mourners* (University of Notre Dame Press, 2021).

www.ingramcontent.com/pod-product-compliance
Lightning Source LLC
Chambersburg PA
CBHW021231020726

47498CB00008B/2794